This book is dedicate  en:
Everything I would like tc ht time

With grateful thanks to
Jo, Barry, Bill and Dee.
Without whom this book would not have come to fruition.

"Remember that if you want carrots don't plant turnips"

Copyright © 2018 Caroline Adcock

All rights reserved.

ISBN:
ISBN-978-1-7200-5094-0:

ME FIT: MENTAL FITNESS TRAINING –
A Handbook for Life

What's all this about?

Modern life is full of ideas and methods to improve physical fitness and the health of the body. This has generated a huge amount of research and investment across the globe, yet most of us allow our minds to do their own thing, with very little attention given to achieving improvements in mental health and fitness. Attitudes about how to achieve mental health in modern society are sketchy and inadequate. We have very little idea about how to cure our worries, shortcomings, bad habits and regrets, and even less on how to use effective methods to lead healthier and happier lives. Why remain a victim to all the ills which befall us simply through ignorance and lack of application? If we really do want to shift our direction of travel some serious efforts will be needed to change the way we live our lives today.

This book is all about introducing a watching brief over our mind by becoming more aware of how important thoughts are in shaping our experiences, our health and our sense of well-being. It provides a simple explanation and rationale for a number of different techniques, with exercises on how we can use them to good effect as part of our everyday life.

There is nothing new or clever about these ideas, and there will be much in this book that you recognize already; it's just basic common sense, a phrase which is often used to describe what the majority of us would like to think we might do in any particular situation based on social norms and accepted wisdom. However, it's very easy for even this basic rule of thumb to go out the window when the emotions take over. Putting a structure in place, together with timely reminders for regular practice, is the proven method for achieving physical fitness so why not do the same in order to achieve mental fitness?

All forms of discipline and training require a sustained effort. This handbook is here to help you and with patience and effort you will succeed.

Once we realise the power which thoughts can have over our well-being, and how easily they colonise our minds, we will want to do something about them. Awareness means that choice becomes possible, and we can decide whether we live in a weed infested field or a beautiful garden.

Mindfulness is a popular idea these days but I'm not sure if people really understand what mindfulness is all about and how they might achieve it. There is certainly an attraction in the idea of living in the moment and maintaining a calm and serene approach to life without being knocked off balance by unwelcome events. However, emptying the mind of thoughts is a challenge for western societies, where the accolades are given to those who take action in order to be successful.

Getting to where we want to be is often about going out and competing or conquering. Our culture puts value on acts of heroic achievement without really weighing up what the consequences might be.

The ME FIT programme adopts a more pro-active approach in order to achieve that same sense of tranquility, but uses a method more in tune with the path which so many follow today in order to improve their physical fitness. Many of the exercises and techniques outlined in the following pages can be adapted to suit individual needs and lifestyles, and I would encourage everyone to keep a notebook and record their responses, solutions and ideas for practice.

Once the journey begins there is no stopping and one idea will inevitably trigger another. Here's to the process and the transformative power of positive thinking.

Chapter and Section Headings

CHAPTER ONE: THINK AGAIN

1.1   The Penny drops

For most of my life I have thought of myself as a rather emotional person. I would have good days and bad days. The good days were those when I found myself humming a tune, dreaming up plans for the future and feeling that I was OK. The bad days were torture and left me feeling screwed up and anxious inside, unwilling to make the effort to meet up with friends for fear of comparing my lot with theirs, hiding from a sense of inadequacy and, at times, coping with a vortex of dread which suddenly grabbed at my insides when I remembered the latest fear I was trying to keep at bay, and not always successfully.

One day I realised that I had a choice. I didn't have to let the bad feelings take over when things weren't quite going my way. Nine times out of ten I believed that action was needed by someone or something before I could feel happy again.

Then it became clear that there was no point in moping around feeling awful if other people were not going to change. Nothing I could do or say would make any difference. They would continue to be the same, regardless of my responses, whether they wanted to or not. At that point I began to realise there was something I could do: A way to feel better. I made a pledge with myself to make every day a good day. Bad days were only there because I allowed them to be. It wasn't easy at first. I had to keep watch every time I slipped into negative mode and make a real effort to challenge the deluge of bad feelings, ready and waiting to pour in to fill the void at every opportunity.

Once I began to introduce some control over my thoughts, and what I allowed in, I began to feel better. Not instantly of course; there was a very gradual improvement day by day. I could still be knocked off my perch in an instant, and it was generally the same old issues which kept tripping me up.

I began to recognize them as my Achilles heel;

something which most people will also recognize - the trigger which strikes at the pit of your stomach in an instant and knocks you to the ground the moment the phone rings or you get wind of the threat which you had thought you had buried once and for all.

But each time I remembered my pledge I started again, and each time I did it got easier. Gradually the deluge of anxieties became a stream; and then the stream was no more than a trickle. The effort involved in turning off the tap became much easier and the benefits I felt were more than enough to keep me on the right path. My health improved; I slept better and woke refreshed. Relationships settled down and became much more harmonious and easy going. I was able to be myself without worrying about what other people were doing or thinking about me, and I didn't worry about what they were doing or thinking either.

The funny thing was, once I stopped worrying about other people and feeling bad about what the world had done to me, or I had done to the world, the problems I was worrying about began to disappear. Suddenly they didn't seem to matter so much. I had a new sense of freedom. I was in control. I realised I could be happy most of the time, instead of those fleeting moments snatched from a sea of negativity.

Shortly after this another penny began to drop:

There is nothing more stressful than being given responsibility for something or someone you have little control over. It's true that responsibility can be seen as an exciting challenge but even so, challenges can still be a form of stress, with all the same consequences for an individual as problems, and after a while over exposure to any form of stress takes its toll.

Can you think of a time when you were given responsibility for something or someone and had little idea how to do it and what the consequences might be?

We have all been through childhood and experienced facing new challenges for the first time. No doubt your blood pressure went up, your thoughts started racing and your routines were messed up.

Remember the relief when the task was completed or someone else stepped in and took over. That same sense of relief is evident when you realise that you are not responsible for other people. I am talking here about adults and those able to make decisions for themselves. It's true that you can offer help, advice, suggestions, love and support but at the end of the day they are the ones to take action, not you. It doesn't matter if you are close to them, or if they rely on you to sort out their problems. They must choose their own direction whilst you can do nothing more than let this happen and accept the consequences. The only responsibility you have is to yourself. Why not be the best that you can at any moment in time and stop trying to control the rest of the world. It's a huge burden and a total waste of energy so drop it now and see how much lighter you feel.

After putting these ideas into practice for a month or two I realised something momentous for the first time in many years. No longer was I an emotional person, or should I say a person governed by my emotions, emotions which inflict pain and suffering rather than joy and happiness. I still had emotions and feelings but I was able to choose the ones I wanted and not let the negative ones control me. The pennies had finally dropped. I realised that there was a similarity between improving my mental fitness for life through discipline and rigour, and carrying out a training programme to build physical stamina and become an athlete. Why had it taken so long for me to realise it?

Does this sound appealing to you? I hope so as this book is written with the aim of helping you to improve your own mental fitness through training so that you can withstand the storms of life by getting your emotions toned up and under control.

The world is not an easy place to deal with and no one escapes pain, disappointment and loss, plus a host of other dark feelings which humans are destined to experience at some stage in their lives. The secret is to build up your mental stamina in order to minimize the suffering which these emotions can inflict.

Old habits are notoriously hard to break and many of us have never thought about changing the way we think any more than changing our name or our ethnic background. However, if you are interested in attempting this path you must sign up to a willingness to make the effort to do so. It is likely to be a gradual process; constant monitoring of thoughts will only become a lifetime habit with practice, and you need it to become so ingrained that it becomes an automatic response.

The benefits will be huge and are likely to result in a significant increase in your sense of well-being and happiness, strengthening your ability to overcome or deal with many of the conflicts which you might be experiencing today.

Difficult times are impossible to avoid but if we are trained up and ready we can more easily accept them and have the confidence to know that we will bounce back.

You will also be a person who is much more useful to others than you are now. The world is in urgent need of a few more "rocks" and you are destined to become one of them if you put these ideas into practice and incorporate them into your daily routine.

1.2   Addicted to Emotion

Emotions are a strange thing. When you think about it they are simply the consequence of thoughts which trigger electrical charges in the brain.   These charges stimulate the nerves which send messages to the cells telling them to release chemicals into the blood.   The chemicals or hormones cause a response in various parts of the body which are fed back to the brain and this registers in our consciousness as an experience of pain or pleasure, in other words, what we call an emotion.   Most of the time it is hard to pinpoint our feelings as they may include a range of emotions which are all mixed in together and difficult to describe.   However, more extreme emotions have obvious signs, such as a tight feeling in the chest, butterflies in the stomach, shaking hands, or blurred vision. Really powerful negative emotions can be devastating and the pain we experience is so uncomfortable we would do anything to get rid of it.   Some people turn to alcohol, drugs and even self-harm, where inflicting physical damage on the body is a more direct and easily explainable pain which can mask or substitute the frightening and overwhelming pain created by the emotions.

Positive thoughts also trigger emotions and these result in pleasurable feelings; we might describe ourselves as being light as air, glowing with energy, relaxed and warm.   The whole range of reactions are caused by chemicals which have an effect on the systems of our body and these reactions create a sensation of pain or pleasure.   They have all been triggered by thoughts.

The strange thing is, we can experience these emotions as a result of our thoughts, whether these thoughts are about what is actually happening to us right now, what we remember happened in the past or even what we imagine might happen in the future. The body cannot tell the difference and simply reacts to the thoughts, whatever might be happening outside in the real world.

When you realise this it becomes obvious that what we allow ourselves to think is absolutely critical to our well-being, and even who we think we are.

It may bear little resemblance to the real world as each person lives in their own reality. That's a pretty amazing idea.

If you think about it the world we see is actually the world we already know projected outwards, and everybody's vision is different depending on their previous experiences.

A person who is a worrier is constantly living in an emotional state where certain repetitive or negative thoughts trigger chemical reactions which have an effect on the body and this is felt as pain or anxiety. Similarly, someone who thinks that the world is a good place, and likes to laugh and see the funny side of things, may experience a lot more pleasure due to their positive thoughts, subsequent chemical reactions and associated emotions.

After a while these responses become habitual and we don't even notice them. It's just the way we are. There is nothing wrong with feeling emotion, even negative emotion. Without emotion we would never have evolved to be the intelligent and functioning human beings that we are. Every emotion has a value, and the feedback mechanism which kicks into action results in pleasure or pain, giving us a guide as to what we should do next and how we should meet the challenges facing us. An emotional person is not a badly functioning one, even though their more extreme emotional responses may get them into trouble at times. The real problems begin when we let one emotion, usually a negative one, dominate over all the others, and for no purpose other than the fact that it has become a habit.

The more that our thoughts trigger familiar emotions the more our body gets used to its daily dose of chemicals which circulate in the bloodstream, providing us with the feelings which describe who we are. The term "adrenalin junkie" is a typical example of the need to maintain the high that some of us have come to know and love.

Take away or reduce these chemicals and the body starts to crave that same cocktail of chemicals which make us feel a certain way.

Feeling that way is how we perceive ourselves to be. It's what we would describe as our personality, and we identify with it so closely that we become trapped in habitual patterns of behaviour and don't believe we can ever be anything different.

Anti-depressants are just one way of changing the chemical mix but it would be much better if we could find another way to do this without the harmful side effects.

This addiction to our emotions goes some way to explain why domestic abuse is such a trap and so hard to break out of. If the environment which triggers familiar thoughts is changed instantly it is not always so easy to deal with the loss of the familiar, a habit which is hard to break. Then the change brings a host of new feelings and emotions which can be confusing, overwhelming and just plain frightening, even though the majority of us would think how much better it must be to be away from the source of pain in the outside world.

Habit is a powerful thing and if we no longer have the familiar sense of who we are a form of panic can set in. We may fear the loss of self and cling on to what we know at all costs, resulting in an even more intense pain than the one we might wish to escape from.

In fact, habit is another name for this addiction and is nothing more than a craving for the familiar.

There is also the fact that once we have learned to think a certain way we keep on doing it until something changes. Patterns of behaviour are stored up and then fired into action when the signal is given. This means that energy is saved and disruption is minimal since everything runs like clockwork. I bet that most of you can ride a bike and if so you will know how easy it is to pick up and start pedalling, even if you haven't done it for years. There is hardly any need to think about what you do as you automatically find yourself just doing it.

Responding to situations in life is much the same. Your thoughts are triggered in a familiar pattern which sets off the same old emotions releasing a similar cocktail of chemicals, creating the same old responses and feelings before you have even started to think consciously about whatever might be happening to you. "Old habits die hard" is a well-earned phrase.

Since emotions are all about chemicals in the body they are no different from any addiction which comes from a regular drug habit like cocaine, heroin, alcohol and even nicotine.

Once your thoughts become repetitive patterns they generate chemicals which create habits and habits are addictive. Keep a check on those habits before you get hooked!

The similarity between emotions and drugs does not end here. I'm sure you have all witnessed how strong emotions can result in people acting in strange ways, often totally out of character, doing or saying things which others would describe as mad. There is no point in arguing with someone who is in a rage. The best thing is to leave them to it until they settle down and come to their senses. They are unable to reason until the storm of emotions has died down. Some people allow their emotions to rule them and once this happens their thoughts are driven by the strength of their feelings. We say that they were not thinking straight, in fact they cannot access any thought other than that which gives justification to their feelings. Large parts of the brain just shut down in these highly charged situations and more primitive responses are allowed the upper hand. This is what is known as the "flight or fight" mechanism.

1.3   Trains of Thought

A better description than the title for this section might be "chains of thought" as this is a very simplistic explanation for the way in which thoughts enter into our consciousness. It's never easy to empty the mind and still be aware – in fact it's virtually impossible for the ordinary human being, and so far I've never met anyone I could call extra-ordinary.

Thoughts have an energy all of their own and sometimes it takes a good deal of effort to keep them from surfacing in our mind, especially when they carry a strong force. This may be because they have powerful feelings associated with them which result in pain and distress, so we need to work hard to keep them suppressed.

Have you ever noticed that when you start to think of one thing, a hundred thousand other things start popping up in your consciousness like images on a screen? There is usually a reason why these particular thoughts come to mind and they tend be linked in some way. We might use this ability to link thoughts together by going back over old ground to remember what we were planning to do when we entered a room, or using each letter of the alphabet to try and remember someone's name. This linking mechanism is a very useful process and it's something we can make use of in the training exercises to improve our mental fitness.

Linked thoughts usually come to us uninvited and we make of them what we will. Some thoughts we put aside and forget all about, may be they don't even register in our mind. Others we may be much more interested in and we pick them up and focus on them more closely. Our consciousness is nothing more than a lens, allowing us to look at something in more detail because it has particular relevance to us and therefore we are interested in finding out more. When we are asleep we drop the lens and all the energies of our thoughts play out in our mind in a haphazard and crazy way since there is no conscious selection or editing taking place.

If a thought appears to be really interesting or significant to us it's heightened by our attention and this gives it greater energy.

The highly charged thought then stimulates an equally high response or electrical charge, exciting the nerves to stimulate cells which release the emotional chemistry resulting in feelings of pain or pleasure. I bet you can easily remember all those moments in your life which are associated with a powerful emotional charge, whereas a host of factual ideas tend not to stir up any particular feeling or emotion, even though they may be important in other ways. Once our emotions are truly engaged the feedback is strong and this charge is etched in our memory like a big heavy brush stroke. It stores a charge which can be triggered many times over whenever a thought links to it. Post-traumatic stress disorder is the consequence of highly charged experiences coming back repeatedly into our consciousness whenever a linked thought triggers them, even one which appears to be irrelevant, such as a particular sound or smell.

Another reason why certain thoughts enter the mind more easily is because of the mood we are in. As you know, "like attracts like" and this couldn't be more true when it comes to our thinking processes. If you are down in the dumps you are only aware of depressing thoughts, whereas a high mood attracts creative and exciting thoughts and ideas. Some people are more prone to mood swings than others; a manic depressive personality can be extremely creative during a high but the individual will pay for it, with very low energy and a sense of doom during a low.

Many people have no idea that this process is taking place and make little effort to control it. We are all ignorant to some extent, and most of the time we allow ourselves to be led by our thoughts without a backward glance. It is so much easier, once you recognize the signs, to stop, look around at where you are heading and start to apply some diversion techniques to steer you around the impending crash.

If we recognize that this is happening in our own mental world we may not be able to do anything about it straight away, especially if we are under the influence of strong emotions, but we can learn to become more aware and recognize the signs at an early stage.

This will give us more leeway to apply the brakes before the train gathers speed, attaching more and more negative thoughts and hurtling down hill towards a mental health crisis.

Once you have lost the immediate connection with a thought, or more accurately a collection of linked thoughts, they have entered your subconscious and are stored there, waiting for a new stimulus to re-energise them and fire off the electrical charge which sets in motion the whole process of feelings which we discussed before. These thoughts also have an energy or charge of their own, which is difficult to access and therefore change. You have to be patient and wait for them to surface in order to deal with them. Once they show themselves, and you are aware of the process, you can replace them with something which is more positive. The stronger this new thought the more it can replace the old and unhelpful response, leaving these negative thought energies to simply wither away.

It's only when our thoughts enter the spotlight that we make anything like a rational or "thought out" decision. Even then, much of the thinking process is simply justification for what we already feel about something because it's nearly always our feelings which matter most, not dry old facts. Our quality of life depends on it.

People who have got used to thinking a certain way and simply accepted it have become acclimatized to their habitual patterns of thought and associated emotional state. Perhaps you recognize someone who has a problem with body odour; everyone else can smell them but they are oblivious. People can find it very difficult to change their thought patterns for two main reasons: They cannot access and re-programme their old thoughts since these have slipped into the subconscious and are out of reach; They have no memory, recognition or awareness of anything new and different which might replace the old thoughts and stimulate feelings which enable them to feel better.

A feeling of openness and trust in the process is essential, especially if you think nothing can change. I would encourage all of you to embark on these exercises with this attitude in mind.

We are all captives of our own subconscious and have adapted to a very specific emotional climate. Unless there is a conscious effort to move out of this we tend to stay in our comfort zone and don't even notice the glorious sunshine outside.

1.4   Before we Begin

This is not another self-help book which promises to sweep every problem out the way and provide a smooth road ahead. I cannot reassure you that there will be no obstacles in your path, no mountains which you must climb, no jungles you have to penetrate and no rapids you must manoeuvre. Life will be what it has always been. The one thing I can promise, however, is that if you carry out these exercises with the best of intentions and put your energy and will behind them you will improve your mental fitness, and thus deal more easily with the challenges ahead. The climb may even become easier as you get used to it and when you get to the top the view maybe worth it!

Nothing is more important in life than getting some control over our thoughts. It does not mean that we lead a rigid and emotionally cold and boring life or that everything will suddenly change overnight. We won't become a distant person who is less involved in what we are already doing. It just means that we keep a check on our thoughts and plan our route before allowing them to run away in whatever direction they take us. It also means regular and constant awareness and re-adjustment to make sure we are not letting the negative thoughts take over, forcing out the positive ones.

Many people find a regime or discipline is a useful step in setting this in motion. The physical discipline which athletes undertake is proof of what can be achieved with constant effort and attention to detail. Their training programmes are rigorous and include diet, exercise, practice and, above all, commitment.

A similar process has therefore been adopted in achieving mental fitness and the format of this handbook is very much like a physical training programme.

Each chapter focusses on a particular theme and includes various ideas to assist reflection on the theme, together with two exercises to help this process.

Time and effort are required over a sustained period if you want to build up your fitness level and maintain it.

The quick exercises are designed to do on your own, ideally on a regular basis, whereas you may find it easier to do the in-depth exercises in a group, or once in a while, as they are slightly more complex and involved.

Why not get together with a few friends to try out some of the in-depth exercises and share your findings?

I recommend working through the book slowly, giving yourself time for reflection between each exercise. Ideas need time to sink in and attempting too many in one go might give you analysis paralysis.

Once each chapter has been dealt with in this way it may be useful to set up some form of mental circuit training to include some or all of the exercises, combining or adapting them in such a way that they meet the challenges in your own life. One exercise from each chapter is a good way to start your training programme. These should be done on a regular basis in order to maintain a firm commitment to healthy attitudes. When you get really involved you may find that this sort of thinking becomes a part of your life and you only need the odd reminder to keep these healthy patterns at the forefront of your mind.

Feedback loops are an essential process in the dynamics of the universe and are built into every single thought and action, whether conscious or not. It's possible that intelligence is simply another word for the way we respond to feedback. Those who practice mental fitness regularly will be more open to change and will respond more effectively to feedback. Those who repeat the same old patterns will eventually be dinosaurs.

Feedback on progress should give you encouragement so compare the way you feel as time goes by. A useful way to do this is to keep a log and score your feelings from 1-10, with 10 being the maximum or best that you hope to feel and 1 being the worst.

All the ideas outlined in this book are not new and I'm sure that anyone who reads them could add their own interpretations and ideas based on personal experience and cultural background.

The important thing about any idea, however, is that it stimulates a response which resonates with the individual, who has the freedom and ability to use their own discernment to reflect on the meaning of the message and decide on their own truth.

Readers are therefore invited to add their own reflections and set up their own exercises which can be changed to suit individual needs as time goes on. Keep a notebook to hand and jot down any ideas and comments which come to mind.

We are all in charge of our own destinies and every attempt to decide on what is right and wrong for each of us is going to be subjective. It depends on the point at which we are at as to where, how and when we view the issues and what decisions we make at the time. Each point of view is inevitably going to be limited and inadequate. It will be different for each person according to the specific time and environment they are in, and we always have the freedom to change our mind. Viewpoints will be different so the truth is a fluid concept which is shaped according to circumstance. There is nothing wrong with being different; diversity is an essential part of creation.

This book is only for those who believe change is possible. Don't try any of these exercises if you insist that the world outside is beyond your control as you will be wasting your time and getting even more frustrated and angry.

Belief is the first step in the process, but belief is nothing more than hope, and hope can soon disappear when the going gets tough.

The Me Fit exercises, practiced regularly with a belief in change, allow us to actually experience change for ourselves. Living the experience means we will know, and knowing is the basis of our relationship with everything that is. Knowing makes us who we are today, and knowing leads us to where we will be tomorrow.

Every experience is valuable as it teaches us more about the mechanics of reality. Nothing is wrong, nothing is wasted, so we can never make a mistake.

We may not like the consequences of our actions but we will only know this by the feelings we experience. Knowing we can bring about change means that whatever circumstance we are in we know what we want, so the direction of travel is in our hands.

Any change, especially if there is a need to shift a long standing habit, requires work as a sudden desire for change, no matter how strong, is unlikely to succeed. Try telling a depressed person to cheer up and you will know how difficult it is to change your mental outlook overnight.

What matters most is the process of change and the journey it takes us on. Getting started is going to be the first step and once this gains momentum, the adventure begins.

Above all, have fun, don't take it too seriously and enjoy the trip.

1.5   First things First

Before we move house, start a new job or undertake a major new project we tend to have a clear out. It's a good time to get rid of all those unwanted items which tend to accumulate and gather dust. They take up valuable space and yet we rarely give them a moment's thought until we are faced with the prospect of moving or losing them.

Why is it that many of us find it difficult to get rid of things? We haven't used them for years and yet the idea of parting with them is a struggle.

The same applies to the ideas and attitudes stored in our minds, and now that we have embarked on a new and healthier regime it may be a good time to reassess what's important for our life and what we can get rid of. Let's make some mental space in readiness for all those bright and shiny new ideas we are about to introduce. Here are some important points to keep in mind -

- **Have faith in yourself and believe that you will always attract what you are looking for;**
- **Be willing to let go when it's no longer useful; that way you will always have space to welcome in the new.**

Let's take stock and look at the clutter that is filling up our mind. We are going to have some fun chucking it out.

CHAPTER TWO: GETTING READY

2.1   Keeping it Under Wraps

Many people consider that their actions are all important and what they think about doesn't count as long as they keep these thoughts to themselves. In many cases people live from day to day believing that what comes into their mind just happens, without any idea as to how that might be linked to all the other things they have experienced in the past. As a result they make no attempt to control these thoughts. They are caught up in the current and tossed around, looking on helplessly whilst being pulled in every direction as a result of a constant stream of thoughts which stir up feelings and emotions.

These uninvited thoughts and images may trigger memories which hold a strong emotional charge and the feelings they generate start to gain energy and may even run riot, leaving a trail of devastation in their wake, influencing all aspects of life in much the same way as a hurricane wreaks havoc on a storm hit country.

You are probably going to say that things happen to us which cannot be avoided. They are enough to knock anyone off balance and the emotional storms which ensue cannot be avoided. This is true, and no-one should underestimate the fact that we are all human and all subject to a huge number of influences over which we have very little control.

The way we experience life is through our consciousness, which is nothing more than thoughts and emotions and the subsequent actions which follow on from these. This constant interplay of thought and action is what drives life forwards and most of the time we haven't a clue about the mechanics. We simply accept the process without question.

If you stopped for just a few seconds you would notice that thoughts are extremely powerful and can have consequences which change the world. Nothing happens in life without an idea or thought preceding it.

Every thought has an energy or charge, and these thoughts must be released in some way as they obey the laws of physics, meaning that nothing is wasted and everything is in a constant state of flux.

If we do not discharge the energy we are constantly under its influence. If the thoughts are ugly and aggressive and directed outwards they can have unwanted influences in the outside world. However, if these thoughts are not released and directed inwards they can act like a poison to those who store them up. Failure to discharge often results in anger, depression, anxiety and mental illness. These negative energies are turned against the self and can intensify. Once these thoughts get a grip they can grow in energy and influence. Many people do little to stop feeding them but allow them to run rampant, with consequent ill effects on their lives.

If we take charge and start to become more aware of our thoughts, and the way that they make us feel, we can begin to take control. This gives us the power to starve out the damaging thoughts and allows more positively charged images and intentions to grow. Good actions and outcomes will naturally follow.

What thoughts do you keep in your mental bank? Is it full of dark secrets and powerful revenge or do you keep the door open and allow the light to come in so you can see what's happening and take the necessary action to prevent damage to yourself and others.

Keeping it Under Wraps – Putting it into practice

KEEP IN MIND
- Nothing happens without an idea or thought preceding it.
- Thoughts trigger emotions which affect how we feel.
- What we are experiencing in the present produces the same emotions as what we remember from the past or imagine in the future.
- Every thought has an energy or charge which must be released. Keeping thoughts locked up can have damaging effects with negative consequences for our mental health.
- Be aware of this and observe what you allow to occupy your mind. Take an active approach; starve out negative thoughts and encourage positive ones.

Quick Exercise:
- Think back over the last few days and see if you can identify any worry or concern which keeps coming into your mind for no obvious reason. Maybe you are busy doing or thinking about something else when it happens. Perhaps it's the first thing you think about when you wake up in the morning or just before you go to sleep at night?
- Notice the feelings which go with these thoughts.
- What do you do when these thoughts come into your mind?
- Make a conscious effort to sort through these thoughts; allow and accept the negative ones but don't dwell on them as they will only grow bigger. Focus on positive feelings and let them fill the space instead.

In Depth Exercise:
- Take a sheet of paper and draw a large circle covering most of the page. This represents a back pack in which you carry around all the ideas, aspirations, worries and concerns which take up space in your mind, whether you want them to or not.
- Inside the circle you are going to draw a number of simple shapes to represent these items or themes. Don't try too hard to include everything but be honest with yourself and include all the

unwanted thoughts as well as the good ones. Remember that this is a snapshot of your bag today; next week's luggage may well be different.

- What do these shapes look like and how much space does each one take up? Give each shape a title. Is it large or small; heavy or light; soft or hard; does it have a colour? Maybe your mental space is full of mists swirling around; maybe you have big heavy shapes which blot out everything else. If you are not sure how to draw your thoughts try and capture what comes into your mind uninvited and how you feel when it does.
- What do you need to keep in your back pack for the journey ahead? Choose what is going to be most helpful to you and get rid of all the useless stuff which is weighing you down.
- Pack only what is necessary to allow you to get to your destination and throw the rest out.
- Check your mental back pack at the start of every day and make sure you have only what you need. Keep it handy and use it to the full.

2.2   Bank of Life

Sometimes we keep hold of negative thoughts because we want to get our own back for the pain and suffering inflicted on us. We feel justified in seeking revenge so we store up the power of our anger, waiting for the day when we can release it to cause maximum damage to those who have hurt us. It isn't fair that someone is allowed to go scot free and enjoy their life when we are left crushed, humiliated and unable to move on.

Unfortunately we can't keep these kind of thoughts under wraps and sealed tight.   They leak out and the poison starts to contaminate all our other thoughts, which causes serious damage and affects our mental health.

Let's imagine that we all have a bank in which we keep our thoughts. People have a tendency to save up their issues and resentments, often in a miserly fashion, and they may reach a point where there's no way they would be willing to part with their large store of grievances unless they get something significant back as a form of recompense. This sense of justice is a huge driving force in all forms of life. It's behind all wars and is a major obstacle to moving forwards and being happy. Until the person holding these grievances is willing to discard them they will sit there growing bigger and bigger until they have filled up their mental space like an ugly growth. Parting with them becomes much harder as these thoughts take root. They push out or starve thoughts which trigger positive feelings and leave the person believing the world is an ugly place.

Ask someone to throw away their negative thoughts and that could leave them feeling empty and bereft. They would no longer have validation, a label which gives that person a sense of being something or someone with a purpose, rather than a nothing or a no-one. The longer and more entrenched these negative thought patterns become the harder it is for that person to throw them out and give space to more positive images.

Sometimes people are very good at putting on a front; they may appear happy and positive, with negative thoughts safely stored away in the vaults of their subconscious.

The effects of these poisonous energies can build up over time however, often emerging in more challenging times when the pleasures of life do not provide sufficient reward or energy to keep the bad thoughts down. Their meagre store of positive thoughts is no longer enough to restore well-being and the consequences may present in lots of different ways; the person gets angry or upset at the slightest provocation, they pick on someone or something with little justification for their rage or simply feel anxious and depressed without knowing why. When this happens most people will no longer be able to make the connection between their negative thinking, established over a long period of time, and the way they feel now. It's just something which has happened to them for no obvious reason. What actually takes place is that the trigger has simply allowed a huge damn of negative energy to overflow and the person has no means of controlling it.

Having said that there is nothing wrong with an effective outburst of well-deserved anger, especially if it results in a good shake up to get rid of the dust. Problems are much more likely to occur when this energy is disguised or locked up and not allowed to vent itself naturally.

In order to prevent the process of negative thought patterns accumulating and building up over time it's important to appreciate the link between hanging on to angry thoughts and the subsequent damage it does to our mental and emotional health. Discipline and training are required to minimise their effects in much the same way as we need to look after our bodies through diet and exercise. A lifetime of junk food and toxins will inevitably take its toll and much the same applies to our mental health. Arteries get clogged with unwanted deposits causing blockages and preventing the flow of nutrients and oxygen, resulting in damage to healthy tissues, poor health and even death. We are only too aware of this and spend much time and energy avoiding these conditions. Mental health is no different and much more awareness is needed to ensure positive thoughts keep the energy flowing freely,

If you find that you have accumulated a store of resentment and anger there is nothing to stop you having a good clear out.

Throw away all those ugly feelings and you'll feel a lot better. They are not going to bring health and happiness, quite the opposite in fact.

Bank of Life – Putting it into practice

KEEP IN MIND
- **The energy locked up in negative thoughts always leaks out; we can't keep it under wraps for ever. Discharging or changing it in some way is essential for good mental health.**
- **What's the point in saving up for revenge; if you do you will be the one who will suffer the most.**
- **Keep the mind clear and don't store negative thoughts; what we think about is what we become.**
- **Drop the ugly thoughts and make room for the positive ones. We will have more energy to spend on having fun and enjoying life.**

Quick Exercise:
- At the end of each day you are going to check your mental bank account to find out how each transaction added to your investments, what you have spent or let go, and whether the final balance is healthy. How you feel will give you the answers.
- Imagine that all your transactions are thoughts which you experience from the moment you wake up. Some consist of positive feelings and a sense of well-being, whilst others are accumulations of negative thoughts which drain you of energy and result in poor mental health. Everything is accounted for and then stashed away in your portfolio.
- Compare the final balance with your opening balance. What did you add to each of the investments; was it a good day or a bad day? Did you make a profit or did you squander your hard earned resources on feeling angry, jealous or hurt? Can you drop these useless or damaging investments before they consume all of your energy resource?
- Based on your current situation, decide what you need to do tomorrow in order to ensure your balance is healthy. Are you going to invest in positive energy or are you going to continue to add to the negative investments until you are bankrupt?

- Do this each day for a week and then compare your most recent balance with the one you started with.
- If you find that you have done well, give yourself a bonus. Simply storing away positive feelings attracts interest and you will be surprised how your mental bank show a healthy balance until one day you realise you are a wealthy person.

In Depth Exercise:
- Imagine that you have an appointment with your financial adviser and together you are going to review your "bank of life".
- Each of your investments and loans are going to be looked at in more detail, and with the benefit of hindsight. What are the reasons behind each of them and are they still important to you? What do you hope to achieve by keeping them and are they serving you well? Will you accumulate interest or will you find you have to pay interest on the loan? Maybe you would like to increase your successful investments and reduce or drop the bad ones. Perhaps you would prefer to cash it all in and start again.
- Once you have decided where you are going, think about what you need to do to turn things around.
- Do this exercise whenever you feel the need to examine where you are going in life.

2.3   Sharing the Load

Fortunately there are a number of ways which help to discharge negative thoughts and take the pressure away by reducing their energy. Admitting and sharing feelings brings them out into the open, diminishes their importance and reduces the bad influence they can have over our well-being.

When we examine our thoughts in the right company they may have less power, and can even appear futile and unproductive. We are able to move away from their spell and start to look at things differently without the need to hang onto them in order to prove a point.

It's almost as if these thoughts and intentions dissolve when they are brought out into the open by sharing them with others in a supportive environment, especially if we receive positive affirmation and are reminded of our good qualities, or get reassurance that we are all human and liable to make mistakes.

This sounds simple, and appears to be an easy way to avoid falling into the traps which damage our mental health. However, most people find it very difficult to do in practice. It's much more likely that when we experience unpleasant or hurtful feelings we hide or bury them. Perhaps we are ashamed of how we feel, or think others won't like us if they find out, and this will make us feel even worse if we try and explain. It seems much better to ignore them, partly through fear and partly through pride. It's important to understand that our thoughts are not the real self, but simply ideas which we have chosen at random to explain who we are and what we do. They may have entered our mind without a second thought and taken root there. It's only when we can achieve sufficient distance and impartiality that we get enough power to cast them off and make better choices in the future.

Many people need to reach breaking point before they will admit their pain and be willing to open up and share it with another. Besides, it's not always easy to find that rare individual who is understanding, trustworthy and sufficiently impartial to be able to take a non-judgemental view and allow us the space and time to look at where we might be going wrong.

If you really are holding a lot of anger, frustration or self-loathing it's impossible to start these exercises in the right frame of mind. Finding a way to offload some of this energy first is essential before you do anything else, and sharing can be a quick and efficient method. Don't think that you are a failure if you need help from someone else; in fact you are much more of a success if you use what is available to you. Take the opportunity to share your concerns and get rid of negative thoughts by giving yourself the chance to reshape your outlook in more effective and healthy ways. Finding the right person to share your feelings with is important. Friends and family are not always the best option as you will be trying to live up to their expectations by presenting a familiar picture of yourself. Strangers often give you more freedom to explore what is going on in your mind.

Use your intuition and go with someone who "feels" right for you. There are a number of organisations and individuals which offer this.

Sharing the Load – Putting it into practice

KEEP IN MIND
- **Share your thoughts with someone first if you feel ready to burst.**
- **Talking takes the pressure off.**
- **Sensible people use the benefits of talking about their feelings to get their thinking back on track.**
- **You are not a failure if you do.**

Quick Exercise:
- Think back over the last few days and identify something which has begun to niggle you.
  Maybe it is something you said or did which has left you feeling uncomfortable, angry or ashamed and you prefer not to think about it.
- Are these thoughts beginning to affect the way you feel about yourself which is less positive than before?
- Is there a particular person who you think might listen to you and allow you to express these feelings in an open and honest way?
- See if you can find an opportunity to talk to them and then check out how you feel afterwards.

In Depth Exercise:
- Think of all the reasons why you are not pleased with the way your life is going. Is there a particular problem or issue which you have kept to yourself for some time and not shared with anyone else?
- Are you are afraid, ashamed, or unwilling to share it?
- Do these thoughts affect the way you feel about yourself?
- Is there a particular person who you think might listen to you and allow you to express these feelings in an open and honest way? If no one comes to mind there is always the **Samaritans**, a national organisation which offers a confidential listening service 24/7 using a Freephone number **116 123**
- See if you can find an opportunity to talk to them and then check out how you feel afterwards.

2.4   Being realistic

I can't stress enough the importance of being realistic. So many new ideas and attempts to improve our quality of life are rubbished as soon as it becomes clear that they can't provide the magic bullet which allows us to get rid of our problems overnight. Sometimes things have developed to the point where it's no longer possible to turn the situation around or apply the brakes in order to call a halt. We have to gain a much greater understanding about the way life works in order to appreciate when change is not going to happen, when it might happen with a bit of effort, and when a gentle nudge in the right direction might make all the difference.

If you were able to draw a graph to show how all events in life start off gently, gain momentum, reach a point of balance and then run out of steam, it would look like a curve in the shape of a mountain or wave. This is an illustration of the dynamics of change, and knowing this allows us to apply technical solutions in much the same way as a design engineer chooses the right push and pull mechanisms to overcome momentum.

How many of us really appreciate this when we decide to use random ways of trying to bring about change without any idea of how appropriate and effective these methods might be? We often end up bashing our heads against a brick wall, getting angry and frustrated when our efforts come to nothing.

There is no point in blaming ourselves, or the methods we have chosen, if things don't always work out for the best. Sometimes it really is impossible to make a difference and maybe it's important that we don't even try. If the worst thing happens the consequences of our actions maybe unpleasant and we will experience them first-hand. Such an experience is valuable in that it can be very effective in persuading us that we don't want to go there again. Just telling someone is not always enough to act as a deterrent. You have probably heard the phrase "learning from our own mistakes" and there is a good reason why this is so.

Many of you will be reading this book in the hope that you can make changes in your life, get rid of problems and generally feel great.

I am pleased to say that I'm sure you will, but it may not always work out the way you hope or expect. Sometimes the situation will be so entrenched that nothing and nobody can make a difference. We may have reached the top of the mountain and as we coast down the other side the only things before us are the consequences. There is no longer any opportunity to turn things around. A terminal illness, or simply getting old, are examples where very little can be done to bring about a change of course; there are likely to be many more events in life which fit into this category.

An attitude of acceptance is the best way to deal with these situations. Life is like that for everyone at times and there are always plenty of snakes lurking on the game board to bring us down, as well as ladders to give us a sudden boost.

Once we have an appreciation of what is going on, and the dynamics behind it, we can save ourselves a lot of effort and anguish by recognising where to push and when to accept. It's no good trying to scale a mountain in a small city car, we need a four wheel drive, and even then it will only take us so far if the way ahead is steep and rugged. If we have reached the point of no return and find ourselves hurtling down hill even the best brakes won't work.

It's impossible to fully know and understand the dynamics of change as so many factors are involved, many of them unseen. We can only keep an open mind and accept that if we approach things with the right attitude and do our best we can never say that we have failed, only that our efforts were no longer a match for all the other influences working towards an outcome and that this outcome was outside our power.

Being realistic - Putting it into practice

KEEP IN MIND
- Don't expect to find a magic bullet for all situations. The methods we choose to apply will not work every time but that doesn't mean the method itself is wrong.
- Some events are too far gone to be able to turn things around.
- Learn to accept what you can change and what you can't.
- Experiencing consequences first hand can be very valuable.
- Choose a method suitable for the effort required.
- Do your best and recognise that there are many other factors beyond your control which affect the outcome.

Quick Exercise:
- Think of two or three examples of events or situations in life which fit into each of the following three categories:
  Very easy to change the outcome with little effort
  Considerable effort needed to change the outcome
  Impossible or very unlikely to change the outcome
  It's more than likely that events span several categories depending on where they are in the process ie change is easier before momentum has built up.
- Consider what actions, if any, might be needed and when in order to make a difference.

In Depth Exercise:
- Draw three columns on a piece of paper and give each one a heading as follows:
  Not much effort needed to change the outcome;
  Considerable effort needed to change the outcome;
  Impossible or very unlikely to change the outcome.
- Think of situations or events in your life which may be causing you some concern or which you would like to change.
- Decide how you feel about the dynamics of each of these in turn and place them in the appropriate column based on how things are today. It may be that they span several columns.

- If you like you can draw a graph to represent these events and then identify the point where the process has reached.
- Then consider what you might be able to do, if anything, in order to make a difference to the outcome.
- Are there any situations which you feel you cannot change and what do you feel about the consequences?

CHAPTER THREE: FEELING GOOD

3.1 A Big Thank You

Now we have done some serious spring cleaning and got rid of a lot of old and useless stuff in our mental attic, let's start with a warm up and choose one of the most valuable exercises for our "Five a Day" exercise regime. It's one which is readily available and easily understood by most people, whatever their lifestyle, outlook or background.

Gratitude is an important and fundamental building block in achieving happiness. There is nothing complicated about this exercise. All that it requires is for us to take off our old glasses, give them a polish, or put on some new specs which allow us to see things with fresh eyes. Forget all those moans, frustrations, fears and envies; take an affectionate and appreciative view of the world, reminding yourself that this is what you are going to concentrate on from this moment in time. Rephrase judgemental thoughts and comparisons as soon as you become aware of them.

Easier said than done, as our insatiable egos are constantly shouting loudly to be fulfilled, to be noticed, to be better than anyone else, to have what we don't have already – an impossible task as nothing is ever going to keep us happy for long. As a consequence, there are few people these days who hold gratitude at the forefront of their thinking. Dissatisfaction is far more prevalent and today's media encourages the cult of material gain and celebrity status, making us focus on what we lack rather than what we already have. It's more likely to be the glass half empty which describes our feelings rather than the glass half full.

Many people spend their life making comparisons and feeling inadequate or hard done by. They become more and more unhappy with who they think they are and such negativity becomes an aggressive thought towards themself. It may even reach the point where they want to destroy themselves through self-harm or even suicide.

Gratitude can dispel the gloom in much the same way as a candle. It gives us a warm glow inside which lights up everything around it.

I can't think of a better way to get an instant and long lasting high which doesn't cost a penny and never gives you a hang-over.

A Big Thank You – Putting it into practice

KEEP IN MIND
- **Remember the glass half full mantra when feeling negative or envious.**
- **Re-phrase judgemental and negative statements and replace with positive ones.**
- **Use gratitude on a regular basis to get a quick fix. It's the cheapest legal high known to man.**

Quick Exercise:
- Become aware of your thoughts and listen to your inner dialogue.
- As soon as you realise that you feel negative, envious or hard done by, make a conscious effort to stop and replace or rephrase these thoughts with more positive ones. Realise that negative attitudes towards others can be a response to feeling jealous.
- If this is difficult, aim to identify at least three positive things which you know or imagine might be true about this person or situation. Even a chance that it could be true is all that's needed here since we are concentrating on feelings rather than facts.

In Depth Exercise:
- Light three candles and place them safely on a table or flat surface in front of you.
- Take three pieces of paper and write one thing on each piece that represents something which you are grateful for. It could be something personal to you or something very general which everyone can enjoy, like a flower or sunshine.
- Place a piece of paper in front of each candle and spend the next ten minutes thinking about these three things in turn, focusing on what you like about them. Remind yourself how lucky you are to know this item and really appreciate its good qualities.
- You can change the item or items each time you do the exercise if you wish. It's the feeling that counts rather than the thing itself.
- If you don't have any access to candles you can imagine them. Like we said earlier in this book, imagination creates the same effect as the real thing, providing you have knowledge of it.

3.2   There's a child in all of us

If we carried out a survey and got honest answers it would probably show that many people have a low opinion of themselves and are only too keen to criticise who they think they are. Despite this, the same people are often capable of much more generous, affectionate and tolerant attitudes towards their children. They want their offspring to succeed where they failed, and are willing to give them everything possible in order to achieve this. There is a danger, however, that the motivation behind this becomes selfish and controlling, especially if it is against the will of the child. No one can fully control another and any efforts to do so are better spent on working through these exercises to improve the self.

Since most of us are more tolerant and understanding towards children, let's use that willingness to accept and make allowances by using it to help ourselves. If we could stand aside and see the child that is still within us, the vulnerable self which needs love, support and forgiveness, we might be kinder and more understanding towards ourselves, instead of experiencing the constant damaging dialogue of criticism and self-judgement.

We inherited our personality and although, like our body, we can shape it to some degree it's not always what we would choose. It often falls far short of our expectations and can lead us into all sorts of situations with unfortunate outcomes. However, we have been dealt the cards and it's up to us how we play our hand. If we accept our failings and work with what we've got we are much more likely to avoid the negativity and poisonous thinking which comes from dwelling on our inadequacies.

Remembering what it's like to be a child, and knowing that we can still feel like that sometimes, allows us to be much more understanding and supportive of our thoughts and actions. The more we can do this the better. We might even see more clearly where we are going wrong as we will be looking in from the outside with the wisdom of our older self, and with the concerns of a parent.

Don't forget that we can always swop our perspective or role at any time, even if we have never actually reached adulthood or become a parent. When we become aware of all these different aspects of who we are we realise that we have thoughts and feelings which belong to each one, and it depends who is taking the lead at any moment in time. The parent, adult or child is in everyone and when we get to know ourselves better it's possible to hear the inner dialogue between them.

Getting to know the child, adult, parent in each of us gives us more empathy and understanding. Empathy is another word for accepting and merging with something so that we can experience it more fully and therefore gain a better understanding. In a way you are becoming the other and then the other is a part of you, rather than being on the outside and separate. This is the way to feel connected and being connected is what we all long for as it is the only way to achieve happiness.

There's a child in all of us – Putting it into practice

KEEP IN MIND
- There's a child in all of us which needs our love and support.
- Be kind to this child and listen to its' needs.
- Encourage rather than condemn.
- We are all capable of taking the role of parent and adult as well as child.
- Give each one space, be tolerant and discover that they will then work well together.

Quick Exercise:
- Place an empty chair in front of you.
- Remember yourself as a young child and invite this child to sit on the chair.
- Ask them how they feel about something which you have experienced recently and feel uncomfortable about. The child is always a part of you so they will have experienced it too.
- Notice their response and listen carefully to what they tell you.
- What would you say to the child to make them feel better?

In Depth Exercise:
- Place an empty chair in front of you.
- Remember yourself as a young child and invite this child to sit on the chair.
- Tell your child about the hopes and dreams you had at that age and what you wanted your life to be like in the future.
- Tell them what has happened to you since and what mistakes you think you made or what has held you back from fulfilling your dreams.
- Ask your child what they would do differently in order to fulfil their dreams.
- What would you say to give them encouragement and the chance to succeed?

3.3 "It's such a perfect day"

Some of you will recognise this as the title of a popular song; one which conjures up a great feeling for me, and hopefully for you as well.

Perfect days maybe few and far between, but even if we can only remember one or two in our life we will be transported back in an instant on seeing a familiar sight, hearing a familiar sound or sniffing a particular scent. Suddenly we are reliving the joyous feelings which were created on that day, however long ago. The stronger the feelings, the clearer the image.

Visualisation is a very effective tool and one that we can all enjoy.

It's a process which can also be used to good effect by conjuring up the future in much the same way as we remember the past. Positive feelings are associated with happy times, whether these times are remembered from the past, experienced in the present or visualised in the future. If we think positively about the future, not only do we enjoy similar good feelings now but we even get a chance to shape what happens next.

Imagining the way ahead and giving it a shape means that we start to believe in the story and act as if it was already happening, or on the brink of coming to fruition. The more we consciously think about a clear and detailed picture of the future by experiencing it in the present, with all the excitement, anticipation and belief that it brings, the more it is accepted by our subconscious. Our thoughts create emotions in exactly the same way as something which is actually happening in the here and now. This affects the way we behave, what we choose to do, who we believe we are and the way we present ourselves to the outside world. It also means that everything and everyone we come into contact with starts to believe in it too, and soon the world is delivering just what we expect.

Our actual experiences in life become more and more like the pictures we create using our imagination. Time for note of caution here however; the old saying "Be careful what you wish for" could come true as the more active we become in shaping our future the more likely it is to happen.

"It's Such a Perfect Day" – Putting it into practice

KEEP IN MIND
- Good times are associated with good feelings.
- The way we feel shapes the way we behave and the way we behave attracts experiences which match our feelings. A downward or upward spiral, whichever way you look at it.
- Use the power of the imagination to build up images of perfect days and live them as if they are happening right now in the present. Enjoy the feelings this creates. Our thoughts and emotions don't know the difference between past, present and future.
- Life is a self-fulfilling prophesy.

Quick Exercise:
- If it feels like you are having a bad day, take a deep breath and sing the words to your favourite song. Ideally it should be something which you have found inspiring. Stuck for ideas? I always go back to the well-known Lou Reed song, "Just a Perfect Day".

In Depth Exercise:
- Next time you wake up in the morning don't start agonising over the day ahead. Instead spend at least ten minutes imagining how it feels to be in the moment, living each minute of your perfect day.
  If necessary set your alarm ten minutes early and allow yourself this dedicated time before getting up.
- Run the action forward from the moment you get up and see everything in detail.
- Keep the following thoughts clearly in the forefront of your mind "This is my perfect day. It's going to provide me with all the wonderful feelings I have been waiting for.
  Everything is working out well. Even if I can't influence the way others behave I am dealing with it perfectly. I feel great; the problems may still exist but I'm not in the least bothered about

them. I feel generous towards others as I am the lucky one. The difficult issues will pass and in the meantime they can take care of themselves, it will all come out in the wash."

- Really see all the pictures in your mind like a movie and concentrate on the feelings they bring. The clearer the pictures are the more energy you have to build your future.

- Use this technique on a regular basis and just lie back and enjoy the experience. Every day should start with a commitment to success.

3.4 Luck is where preparation meets opportunity

This is one of my favourite sayings and I frequently remind myself that there is no such thing as luck. Of course there is to some degree, but I would suggest that luck is not quite as passive or elusive as some people think.

We have already talked about how we notice things that have meaning for us and ignore others which we have no interest in. It's a bit like dangling our rod in the sea, well baited for our favourite fish, and hoping for a good catch. With enough rods and the right bait, luck tends to find us, providing we are open to it and ready to accept the responsibilities it brings.

I think that I will leave you to find this out for yourself so here are the exercises to practice. Good luck and see what happens next!

Luck is where preparation meets opportunity – Putting it into practice

KEEP IN MIND
- **Luck is not as random as we think. Use it to achieve success by being prepared to receive it.**
- **Work on getting the mind focussed on positive thoughts, be open to ideas and be ready to snatch the opportunity when it comes along.**

Quick Exercise:
- Think about the people you know and decide who you might call a lucky person and who you might call an unlucky person.
- What characteristics do these people have? Are there any differences between the lucky people and the unlucky ones?
- Do you still consider luck to be entirely random or have you noticed anything which might indicate why someone is more likely to be a lucky person?

In Depth Exercise:
- Choose something which you expect or want to happen in the future. It doesn't have to be anything big or exciting but it needs to be something which you hope will go well.
- Prepare yourself to be lucky. Remind yourself that everything is going to be great and maintain a positive outlook.
- Now fast forward and see yourself living this future as if it was happening now. Be as imaginative as possible; take in all the details, visualise the feelings and enjoy the experience.
- Then put it aside and carry on with your life as before.
- Keep an open mind about what happens next and don't set time limits or lose hope. Luck can take a long time to ripen. Too many people give up and close the door if they don't get an immediate response.
- Keep it to yourself and only tell someone about it when it has happened.

CHAPTER FOUR: FINDING OURSELVES

4.1   Mirror, mirror on the wall

How do we know what we look like? There is an easy way to do this and that is to look in the mirror. The same thing happens when we try and form an idea of who we are, the mirror being the outside world.   Everything around us is constantly reflecting back a response to our existence. The pressure of the chair is a response to our weight, the greeting from a friend is a response to the friendship we enjoy with them and the hate directed at us is often because we represent something which a seemingly hostile world does not like. Everything is relative so the information we receive is unique to us and based on what we present to the world at the time. Other people will have their own reality as they are taking up a different space, presenting as a different self and receiving different messages to confirm this.

A person who feels good about themselves most of the time has generally received a lot of information to confirm that they are OK. It's basically a feedback loop where the messages are constantly reinforced. The more positive we are the more confirmation we receive about the kind of person we believe ourselves to be. Eventually the messages are so regular and strong that they are absorbed into our subconscious, with the unquestioning belief that we are a good person.

When we don't receive a constant message like this it's difficult to make up our own minds about the kind of person we are. Imagine how much harder this is if we are bullied or abused, and spend most of our life feeling vulnerable and at the mercy of mood swings.

Other people have their own agendas and may not be able to give us an unbiased view of ourselves, but their response is the only thing we have to go on in order to know ourselves.

We frequently get mixed messages from the outside world and it can be very confusing. More often than not the information is jumbled and contradictory and as a result the mirror is hazy.

We don't have a clear idea reflected back to us so we are constantly checking what others are telling us about ourselves. Without a clear idea as to who we are we rely even more heavily on other people to give us the answer. This makes us very vulnerable and we go out of our way to seek approval, especially from those we want to be like or who we want to like us. We find ourselves doing things we don't really want to, just to get noticed, or even better, to gain approval. We have forgotten what we need to do in order to please ourselves. This story is all too familiar and at its worst it can be very damaging to our long term mental health.

Sexual abuse is an extreme case, especially when experienced at an early age, because of the mixed messages which the abuser gives to the abused. Abusers tend to choose vulnerable children as these children are often seeking confirmation from the outside world about who they are. They need to be liked in order to feel safe and to get a sense of their own self-worth so they may be reluctant to speak out or cause a fuss. The emotional damage which this causes, accentuated by the powerful impact of the abuse, is the reason why some people are so mixed up in their later years and find it so hard to talk about themselves.

If we run around in a desperate search for approval to boost our low self-esteem we will soon be exhausted. Even worse, we may find ourselves doing anything just to please others by trying to be what they want us to be. If we are teenagers, our parents may want us to work hard at school and be pleasant and chatty with the family whilst our friends encourage us to stay out late, have fun and not stress about schoolwork. How do we keep everyone happy?

The more we run around trying to please them all the more confused we become.

It's very important to take a step back and concentrate on what feels good for us. Block out the judgemental voices of others and concentrate on our own mental dialogue. Be honest with ourselves so we can identify when things feel most comfortable and natural.

It doesn't mean we can do just what we want and ignore sensible advice and help.

We just need to start listening to our own inner voice. The only really important relationship is the one we have with ourselves.

Mirror, mirror on the wall – Putting it into practice

KEEP IN MIND
- How much do we rely on the outside world to tell us what we should feel about ourselves?
- Are we trying to do things just to please others and are these things in conflict? We can never please all of the people all of the time.
- Do the people we rely on to give us good feedback have their own problems; can they see us as we really are or is it their own agendas which affect the way they behave towards us?
- Listen to your inner voice and believe what feels comfortable and right for you.
- The only really important relationship is the one we have with ourselves.

Quick Exercise:
- Think about something you are planning to do, such as getting involved in a new hobby, meeting up with someone, buying some new clothes, or taking a job.
- If you are not sure what to do you may be worried about what others will think and say. Listen to the dialogue in your head. Who is telling you what and how do you feel when you listen to what they say?
- Are they all in agreement or do you find that there are conflicting opinions?
- Tell all the other voices to go away and leave you alone.
- See if you can get a sense of how you would feel if they were silent.
- Listen to your inner voice and what it's telling you. Decide if it feels right for you, regardless of what others are saying.

In Depth Exercise:
- Take a piece of paper and draw a small circle in the centre. This represents you.
- Around the outside draw more circles to represent the main people in your life. Imagine that they are all speaking to you and

voicing their opinions; the bigger the circle, the louder the voice; If you hear one voice a lot, draw it close to your own circle; if it only speaks to you occasionally, draw it on the edge of the page.

- Write down a name against each of the circles surrounding your circle; it can be one person or a group of people. Describe in a few words whether it is a critical or supportive voice or both.
- When you have finished, take a good look at your diagram and see if there are conflicting voices surrounding you. Do they agree with each other? Draw lines between you and the surrounding circles to show who speaks loudest – use thick lines for voices that are strongest and thin ones for those which don't matter so much to you.
- Then think of three positive statements about yourself which come from your own inner voice and write them across the whole of your page in big letters.

4.2   Take the starring role in your movie

Sometimes it's easy to decide what to do in a certain situation by thinking about how someone else might react or behave. Perhaps you have a favourite role model, someone you respect and admire? Ask yourself the question, "What would x.... do in the same circumstances?" A series of images may start to take shape and you can focus on them and allow the vision to play around in your mind like a film. It's surprising how our actions automatically follow on from our thoughts. You may find that the more you think about how that person would behave the more like them you become. You may even start to take on some of their mannerisms, words or ideas. Be aware that like attracts like.

Another important influence is the role which fashions and stereotypes can play in shaping our lives. Perhaps you are a younger person with a keen sense of keeping up with the fashions and trends of the day. Maybe you are an older person who still has a soft spot for a certain era. If we are keen to fit in and be admired by certain groups of people we are likely to find ourselves wanting to be as much like them as possible, wearing similar clothes, sharing the same likes and dislikes, and behaving in similar ways. This occurs without a moment's thought, and blind acceptance of the values of the group reassures us that our choice is clearly the best since everyone else thinks so too. We have bought into the stereotype lock, stock and barrel. This reinforces the values which the group represent to the outside world, the way the world responds and eventually the way individuals in the group see themselves.

Using a role model to shape our own life can be a very powerful thing. It gives us an instant guide on what to do next and how to do it without struggling to answer these questions ourselves.

Be careful however. All role models are only human. They have their own inadequacies and problems and won't necessarily have the right answers for us. No-one is identical and we can never trade ourselves in to become someone else completely.

Some people cling on to these role models for all sorts of reasons.

Change is often unsettling and many people prefer what is comfortable and familiar. Others are very apprehensive about giving up their identity, even if their current role model is no longer useful to them. Fear of what might happen is a big obstacle to change, especially if the role allowed them to survive in a hostile environment by taking on the identity of a group. Sometimes identity becomes so much about what we believe we are today that we can lose touch with our own potential and can only recognise ourselves in a particular, and often limited, role. We are frequently scared that others will no longer see us for the people they believed us to be.

Use this exercise with care and always keep in mind that you are only borrowing a role, not losing yourself in it. Check out how it feels for you and always keep you own judgement and discernment sharp.

Take the starring role in your movie – Putting it into practice

KEEP IN MIND
- Focus on the person, think like the person, act like the person and we will start to feel like the person.
- Use this method with care! All role models are only human. Keep discernment sharp and do what feels right.
- The more we buy into a lifestyle or group the more we find that we blindly accept their values.
- Borrow the role, don't lose yourself in it.

Quick Exercise:
- Think of an argument or difference of opinion you have had with someone recently, especially if the situation is not resolved.
- Choose a favourite role model. Someone you admire and respect; someone who would know what to do and say in this situation so that everything would turn out right.
- Swop over and become your role model. In this new self you imagine that you are sitting in front of the person you had the argument with.
- Notice what you are saying to this person.
- How are you are feeling when you say it?
- How are they responding to you and what do you feel at the end of the conversation?

In Depth Exercise:
- Choose a favourite role model. Someone you admire and respect; someone who always seems to know what to do and how to behave.
- Think of a problem or decision that you are facing in life and are finding it hard to deal with. What are your thoughts and feelings about what might happen next?
- Swop over and become your role model. As this new self you begin to notice how you think and feel about the problem or decision. Decide on a course of action and visualise taking in all the details as the future unfolds.

- Now return to being yourself and re-run the same scenario with you in the leading role, remembering what you have learned from your role model.
- Do you feel differently and what does the future look and feel like now?

4.3 Putting out there what you want to get back

I have often wondered why we tend to have a judgemental and critical view of the world when we are outside looking in. Is it because we are not engaged and therefore have no feeling of connection? The outside world is separate from us and therefore alien and more of a threat. The less we identify with a group of people, the more we lack understanding and a sense of knowing their thoughts. In this situation we tend to feel threatened, seeing them as an unknown and unpredictable enemy and preparing to defend ourselves from attack. A person with a closed mind has a limited understanding of others and is therefore on the lookout for danger round every corner. Our levels of hostility depend on whether we feel part of something or not.

Having a sense of separation is likely to result in a judgemental attitude as anything foreign or unlike ourselves tends to be rejected. It becomes a threat to the ego, whose chief purpose is to maintain and protect the familiar, rather than risking something new.

These judgements are often split second and happen outside our conscious thought processes. In these circumstances the decisions we make are a result of an emotional response to the feeling of separation which we don't question. The messages we give out through our body language, tone of voice, and the things we say and do will reflect our feelings of separation and hostility towards others. They will pick up on this and reflect back the same responses to us. These responses may be as small and insignificant as to be below the radar, but most of us are highly tuned to spot the smallest signals. Even as a baby we respond to facial expression, body language and tone of voice by mirroring the feeling in ourselves and then deciding whether we like this feeling or not.

There are even more factors at play here which accentuate this response.

Once we have aroused certain emotions in ourselves we are primed to notice everything in tune with this emotion.

Maybe you can remember a day when you were feeling down and everything you experienced that day held no excitement or promise. You picked up on the gloomiest news stories. You shared similar tales of doom and gloom with friends and you looked in the mirror with little enthusiasm for what you saw. All the fun and joyous things didn't get a look in as you either failed to notice them or dismissed them as wishful thinking or deluded fantasy.

Everyone has heard of the glass half empty syndrome but let's spend a bit of time looking at the effects of this in our own lives and making sure we reverse the picture and focus on a glass half full.

Putting out there what you want to get back – Putting it into practice

KEEP IN MIND
- Maintaining a positive frame of mind is important as it affects the way we look at the world and how the world responds to us.
- Anything which threatens is seen as separate to us and it feels bad.
- Connections with the outside world are made when we feel involved or engaged, which results in good feelings and a sense of belonging.

Quick Exercise
- When you are about to enter to a busy place, sit down in a quiet spot for five minutes and think about all the things you don't much like about yourself, other people and the world in general.
- Then get up and walk around. Make eye contact or engage with people whilst these feelings are uppermost in your mind.
- Notice how you feel about these strangers, the judgements you make and how you feel about yourself. Then change the exercise:
- Sit down quietly and spend five minutes thinking positive thoughts about yourself and other people. See them as friends and helpmates, get excited about all the ways they may provide a means for you to live in the modern world and all the good things you want to do for others.
- Then get up and walk around. Make eye contact or engage with people whilst these feelings are uppermost in your mind. Notice how you feel about these strangers, the judgements you make and how you feel about yourself.
- Compare the two activities.

In Depth Exercise:
- Think about all the on-going situations in your life, such as where you live, your relationships, jobs, or studies.
- Take a piece of paper and divide it into two columns. The column on the right is your glass half full column where you are going to write down all the positive things about your life.

- The column on the left is your glass half empty column where you are going to write down all the things which are wrong or inadequate in your life.
- When you have finished you may get an idea where your balance lies.
- If it is weighted heavily in the direction of the glass half empty, spend a bit of time rephrasing each of the negative points in turn and finding a way to change them into positives. Add these comments to the glass half full column and draw thick black lines through each of the original comments in the glass half empty column.

4.4   How Does Your Garden Grow?

We generally take reality for granted and become so familiar with it that anything which does not fit with the way we think is viewed with suspicion and doubt. This is a natural reaction, and some people react more strongly than others. You may be one of those more adventurous people who love to explore new ideas and opportunities, but unless you can find like-minded people to share them with you may be ridiculed and made to feel weird and whacky. This can stop us moving forward and pushing the boundaries. It's much more comfortable to be accepted rather than questioned, and safer to simply repeat what we already know.

Creativity and innovation flourish where there is an environment of open minded thinking, with support and encouragement to nurture new ideas, however unlikely or inappropriate they might appear.

Whilst there is something to be said for keeping our feet on the ground and insisting on proof before we believe what others tell us, a closed mind is not much different to the thought processes of a robot, In fact robots and super computers can operate much more effectively than the human brain in dealing with certain mental tasks so why compete? The essence of being human is that we are at the forefront of evolution because we are open minded, curious and able to enquire. For those who want to enjoy the excitement and joy of being creative it's important to keep this in mind, since creativity requires the fertile ground of the imagination to flourish. Those who are locked into existing norms are destined to repeat the same mistakes for ever.

Keeping healthy, both mentally and physically, is essential if we want to keep our mind in the right condition for new ideas and energies to flourish. If we are tired and dejected an idea may appear but is easily rejected as we do not have the appetite to look after it and nurture it. New ideas are fragile things and need constant care. They can easily wither when exposed to criticism or a harsh environment, but will fail to thrive in the dark with no exposure to the outside world.

Most people have a good understanding of how to look after a plant and they appreciate the importance of fresh air, nutrients, water and light. It's a rare thing for anyone to understand how to cultivate ideas and bring them forward with the same scientific rigour as you might use in preparing the ground to produce healthy growth. The mind is very much like a garden and if you want yours to be a place of beauty and productivity you need to look after all your thoughts in much the same way as a good gardener looks after his or her plants.

Remember that truth can be stranger than fiction and there are far more things we don't know about than things we do. All ideas were once thoughts in someone's mind before any proof could be given. They had to be carefully developed and experimented with before others would believe them.

How Does Your Garden Grow? – Putting it into practice

KEEP IN MIND
- **New ideas are fragile things and need care and attention if they are to survive.**
- **Creativity and innovation need the right environment to flourish.**
- **Repeating the past and refusing to consider anything new may feel safe but that's how robots behave.**
- **Truth is often stranger than fiction. There are many more things we don't know about than things we do.**

Quick Exercise:
- Identify at least three things which you are familiar with but have no idea how they work e.g. Radio TV and phone signals
Computers and processors
Aeroplanes
- Imagine you are describing them to someone who has never seen or experienced these things before and notice how they would react.

In Depth Exercise:
- Think of an idea or plan which you would like to carry out. It might be a bit unusual or off beat and you may be worried about looking silly, being criticised for failing to deliver.
- Imagine that you are going to plant this idea in a pot and place it in your greenhouse so you can look after it carefully.
- What things do you need to care for the idea so that it grows well and is able to withstand the harsher climate of the outside world? What will it need to survive and thrive?
- Nurture the idea and when you feel that it's ready, plant it out and visualise it getting bigger and stronger. Show or tell other people about your idea but choose carefully who you share it with.
- See how it's now the best and most unusual thing in your garden, admired by all. Do this every time you have a dream which is ambitious or innovative.

CHAPTER FIVE: TAKING ACTION

5.1 Judge not

This is a big beast and will take a lot of mental muscle to deal with. Are you ready for a good workout?

It's very easy to make an instant decision or judgement in relation to a particular person or situation and once we have done this the doors close and a chain of responses are set in motion.

These responses take us in a certain direction and once these trains of thought begin they tend to reinforce long standing prejudices. The more we hold onto these prejudices the more we repeat them, until the point is reached where a decision takes place below the radar without much input from our conscious questioning mind. One thought simply triggers another, and then another. Before long a huge snowball is barrelling along gathering speed and recruiting strong emotions which give us all the justification we need to feel the way we do. Once these judgements get a grip, further thought is simply justification for the emotions we are already experiencing, despite the fact that these emotions are a response to things that happened in the past. They bear little resemblance to the current situation, which has merely provided a trigger or release for the energies stored up in old ideas or patterns.

A process such as this can be greatly influenced and amplified by the opinions of a group. We have all seen how racism, homophobic behaviour and other prejudices can spread like wildfire. There is a sense of safety in a group, and the need to belong can be so strong that the individual concedes their own judgement and discrimination by buying into the group mind and taking on the values which bind the group.

If we could hold back from making judgements instantly and automatically we would give ourselves more time to think things through. Our decisions would be more rational, based on a better understanding of the person or situation we are facing. This will lead to much less anger and improved mental health.

Holding back from making a judgement does not mean that we are switching off or failing to address a situation if we are still paying attention. Careful analysis will provide a better understanding as to what is likely to serve the situation well and what is likely to cause damage. Taking stock will also allow us to see the reasons why we behave in a certain way, generally as a result of ignorance or habit.

Judgemental responses maybe due to our own conditioning, or they can be generated by fear and a wish to protect our ideas and egos. This can result in a host of negative thought patterns which are often very damaging to the individual, as well as to those we judge. The more fearful we are the more judgemental we can be. Notice how negatively we judge the world when we are feeling afraid or when our sense of well- being is challenged. Then look at how much more open we are when things are going well for us.

Control and exerting power over others is a bullying tactic, often employed by those with an over-inflated ego. It takes a lot of energy to protect this ego, and we may find that we are engaged in a constant battle to ensure that nothing can weaken it.

Be vigilant and notice that the judgements we make are often nothing more than the need to protect a self which is vulnerable and fearful. They serve no useful purpose other than to generate anger and damage to our mental health.

Be aware that the need for control can also be a form of self-protection, rather than an objective view of something which we perceive as bad.

Those who feel vulnerable are particularly keen to protect themselves, but once we develop a strong sense of inner worth we have much less need to fear the effects of outside influences. We become more able to view the so called "bad actions" of others with compassion rather than judgement since we are no longer using our energy to defend our ego.

So many judgements are made on the basis of superficial signs and limited information. We make snap decisions if something doesn't match our own mind set. For instance, it is very easy to feel hostile towards strange religious practices and unusual lifestyles.

When someone or something doesn't fit with the ideas and values which shape who we think we are we feel threatened.

Once this feeling is triggered there is little chance to feel empathy or compassion for the other person. Our priority is to defend ourselves against the alien threat and a power struggle ensues.

Another way to avoid judgement is to encourage empathy and this is all about putting ourselves in another's shoes. We need to bear in mind that the words or actions one person uses to describe or create something is very different to those used by another, even though the feeling behind them could be very similar. For centuries there have been arguments over whether we should worship one God or many. In the end these are only words and ideas which are far too inadequate to really describe the feelings behind what each and every person is seeking, or has a vague sense of. These are abstract concepts which have no words.

Does it really matter what routes people take to experience the same feelings? All that matters is the feelings and intentions behind them. You can get from A to B on foot, by bicycle, train or plane. All very different methods but in the end you arrive at the same destination.

Whilst it is clear that we cannot condone all actions it is much more helpful to try and understand them by putting ourselves in another's shoes in order to seek out how this person might be feeling. Sometimes this can help to remove or reduce hostility and encourage compassion or sympathy.

So let's not get too hung up on the method when it's the result that counts. I am not suggesting that we cheat the system or cut corners to get to same destination. There is no hiding from the truth as far as our thoughts are concerned. Once they are in the subconscious we can't get rid of them that easily. They have a habit of bouncing back, pulling us in different directions unless all our thoughts are in harmony with the bigger picture.

I like the phrase "whatever gets you through the night." As long as it's legal and doesn't hurt anyone intentionally there is something to be said for using what we can to get the end result we are looking for.

Judge Not – Putting it into practice

KEEP IN MIND
- Judgement is often a cycle of snap decisions based on the subconscious repetition of old patterns which produce automatic responses which confirm our prejudices.
- How useful are these old patterns or prejudices to you and those you judge at this moment in time?
- Judgement can also be due to how we feel about ourselves, whether we are vulnerable and trying to protect our ego or the beliefs and ideas which shape us.
- Put yourself in another's shoes to understand where they are coming from.
- It's the end result and the feelings it creates which count, not the means of getting there.

Quick Exercise:
- Next time you are in a crowd of strangers, look around and notice how quickly you make an assumption about each of them. Even the slightest visual signal can lead you to form an opinion without thinking about it.
- Which of the people in the crowd do you feel drawn towards; who would you like to speak to?
- Is there anyone you might prefer to ignore or even avoid?
- Why do you think you might have made these choices?
- Can you link your judgements to any of your own experiences which happened in the past, or to any of the ideas or beliefs which you have about yourself now?

In Depth Exercise:
- Think of someone you have been quick to judge and now have a negative view of. It should be someone you know reasonably well.
- How do you feel about this person and what is it about them which brings out these emotions in you?
- Can you link your judgements to any of your own experiences which happened in the past or to any of the ideas which you have about yourself now?

- Do you know why the person you have hostile feelings towards behaves in this way? Consider everything which you might know about them which could be the cause of this eg their upbringing and past experiences, their social and cultural background, their own fears and vulnerability. Visualise yourself in these situations and get a sense of what they might be feeling.
- Now that you have a better understanding as to why this person acts the way they do, how do you feel about them now?

5.2   Freedom to choose

As a human being we have the luxury of choice, and despite what some people think we have the ability to choose how we respond in each and every moment. It's true that we may not be able to change external circumstances but we can always choose our reaction to the present. Even the slightest difference can nudge our journey towards a different destination; the degree of change all depends on where we are in the journey.

Imagine you are driving a car to work. You are in a jam and wonder why you didn't take the alternative route. Maybe it's too late to take that detour now and you have to stick to the main road. Someone else overtakes you on a motorbike. A bike would have been great but you were talked out of buying one some time ago. Now you wish that you had left the car at home and gone by train; it would have been a lot quicker. Once you have chosen your means of travel and your route there is very little flexibility as to what happens next. If you had made a different choice at the start, however, you could be at your destination by now. You are fretting as you are going to be late. Is there really nothing you can do to get there quicker? Life is a pain.

Most of us live our lives in the present based on the consequence of choices made in the past. We can't change the things that have already been decided but we still waste our energy on being annoyed or angry about them. There is one thing we can always change, however, and that is our attitude to what is happening in the present.

Imagine yourself back in the traffic jam. Do you get angry and end up spending the day in a bad mood, blaming someone or something else for the problem, or do you simply accept that you will be late through no fault of your own, put some music on and enjoy the extra time to yourself? Gradually the choices you make in the present will filter down and start to shape the future.

Arriving at work in a good mood, even though you are late, is likely to have a better outcome than if you arrive angry and fraught. It could mean that you get to start a whole new journey as a result of being a model employee rather than a grumpy one.

Even tiny adjustments nudge you along the path and affect the choices you make each and every second of the day. You can't always see these changes until they add up and you find yourself on a different path. The process is a never ending adjustment based on how we choose to act right now.

Many people become impatient and expect change to happen instantly. It may take a lot longer than you think, and if it doesn't happen straight away the process of taking control and making change happen the way you want it to be is a result of your own thoughts and actions. This is the mechanism which shapes the story of your life. Without the will to change some people will stay in the world of the dinosaurs whilst others will evolve.

Don't expect miracles to happen overnight; it's true what they say, "Rome wasn't built in a day."

Freedom to choose – Putting it into practice

KEEP IN MIND
- Every single moment gives us the freedom to choose how we react.
- Life as we know it today is the consequence of millions of choices made in the past.
- Our attitude in relation to what is happening now is all that matters, not the results of what has been chosen before.
- Sometimes, the smallest step becomes the tipping point and can lead us in a different direction with the biggest change in outcome; on the other hand, it maybe the gradual accumulation of many steps that results in change.

Quick Exercise:
- When you are faced with some minor annoyance during the day which is causing you frustration and stopping things working out in the way you want them to -
- Think about the above example of being stuck in a traffic jam.
- Make the decision that from now on you are going to make choices which allow you to enjoy life whatever happens and banish the feelings of frustration and annoyance.
- Imagine that time moves forwards very gradually and observe how you will react to each moment, given the fact that you have the freedom to choose and have opted for a great future.
- Visualise what happens next and enjoy those positive images of the future.

In Depth Exercise:
- Think about an area of your life where you feel trapped or stuck.
- Based on the scenario of being stuck in a traffic jam, think about how you can react in positive ways whatever situation you are in. Remember that even the smallest change in direction can lead to a different destination but you need to keep up the momentum.
- Visualise life moving forwards very slowly; notice how you are reacting to every little thing. Appreciate that you always have a choice, however small, and identify with the thoughts which feel

best for you. Don't expect or demand big changes overnight but start to build an appreciation of how the small changes can result in something good happening and how much better you feel.

- Do this on a regular basis whenever you feel trapped.

5.3 Never mind the currency, it's what you spend it on that matters

Many people get caught up in the right and wrong way to do things and agonize over the fine detail. This is often the cause of major arguments and disputes, with people falling out and not wanting to communicate with each other as a result.

Arguments over detail are particularly common in relation to religious doctrine and social etiquette. There is a desire to cling on to what is deemed to be right or wrong based on the rules. These rules were often imposed or agreed upon a long time ago and are more in tune with events and people in the past, rather than those of today. Despite this, such rules often feel comfortable and familiar as they allow people to get a sense of being right or wrong without having to think about it. Protecting the details becomes all important in an attempt to keep the status quo, and there is no longer any need to test out the consequences of these decisions and decide whether they feel right for you. At the end of the day we should be searching for the kind of feeling we get from the outcome of any decision or set of rules and not bothering too much about the details.

Arguing over the so called right or wrong methods to deliver the same end result is pointless. There are many roads which lead to home and it maybe that some prefer to take the winding picturesque route whilst others are happy trailing along the main highway.

For many the difficulty comes in not knowing what it feels like to be right or wrong, or even what the end result is supposed to look like. We are so conditioned by the culture and standards of our group that we often hand over the responsibility to someone else and leave society to provide us with the answers. Making decisions is stressful. It requires us to constantly test out our values and our aims in relation to the choices before us.

Another reason for towing the line is that we are social animals and we all have to live together in relative harmony. The pressures on us to accept these rules and go with the majority are huge, and for many they are overpowering.

However, we must also keep our heads above water and make sure we stay awake in order to observe the process, otherwise we simply maintain the status quo through acceptance or by wasting our energy in useless arguments about the detail and decisions about things that don't really matter.

**Never mind the currency, it's what you spend it on that matters –
Putting it into practice**

KEEP IN MIND
- Rules and customs maybe out of date and inappropriate for today's world.
- Many people get caught up in arguing about the detail without thinking about the reasons why. They may have no wish to examine for themselves what feels right and wrong or where they are heading.
- Be aware of the need to live harmoniously with others by observing the rules but question what these rules really mean and how you feel about them before you accept them.

Quick Exercise:
- Think of an argument which took place recently. It can be one which you are involved in or one which you observed.
- What was the argument about and how important were the details?
- Did people get upset about detail and how important did you feel they were to the main issues of concern?
- Why do you think this was so?

In Depth Exercise:
- Are you familiar with a set of rules in relation to your school, college or place of work?
- Do you know when these were drawn up and by whom?
- Do you think these rules are useful and relevant to what really happens in practice?
- Do people obey the rules and how often are they broken?
- Can they be properly enforced and what are the penalties for breaking the rules?
- Could you rewrite the rules to make them more relevant or user friendly?
  Concentrate on the important messages and give less attention to detail.

- If you have time, do a similar exercise in relation to your own life. Write out the rules which you think govern your life today and rewrite them in a way which makes them more relevant to you.

5.4   Choosing the moment

Since everything is constantly in a state of flux changes are happening all the time, even if we can't see them. Many people often feel stuck or trapped and can't see a way out. They are afraid that nothing will ever be any different and they lose heart. If we have no idea about what to do next it's important not to force the issue but to allow events to take their course and then intercept at the right time. We wouldn't pick fruit until it has ripened, but we wouldn't leave it on the branch to rot either. Choosing the moment is very important if we want to achieve success and this means being patient, keeping watch, understanding the dynamics of the situation and not being afraid to take action when the time is right.

Urgency and the "want it now" culture are very dominant in today's world and the need for the adrenalin rush which comes from constant novelty and experience can be very addictive. The advantages of a slower pace are not given much credit.   Many people do not give themselves time to recover from a crisis or set back in their life and think that if they are not on top of their game and fulfilling their dreams every minute of the day they have failed. Nature cannot be rushed and we need to nurture our bodies and our minds, giving them the same respect in order that they may regenerate naturally.

However, it is all too easy to miss the moment and allow it to slip by. One of the biggest excuses for not taking action is fear. It keeps many people rooted to the spot, along with the safety of familiarity and the lack of appetite for change. This attitude is equally as damaging and therefore we need to tread the middle path, being aware of the need for change but choosing a time when it is most likely to be successful for us.

Choosing the moment – Putting it into practice

KEEP IN MIND
- **Allow events to take their natural course.**
- **Balance is important; don't force the issue but be ready to move when the time is ripe.**
- **Be wary of the "want it now" culture but don't let fear and familiarity keep you rooted to the spot.**
- **Practice wisdom by learning to know when the time is right so that when action is taken it is most likely to succeed.**

Quick Exercise:
- Think of your favourite sport, either as a participant or a spectator, and note the following:
- Observe how important timing is. When you act too quickly you fail to connect but equally you experience failure when you are too slow.
- Think of a recent situation when you may have acted too quickly or too slowly and failed to achieve your goal. Consider the reasons why your timing was wrong.
- Visualise what you need to do in order to get the timing right next time.

In Depth Exercise:
- Are you facing any decisions or changes in your life which require action?
- Choose one and fast forward in your mind, using your imagination, to explore what the outcome might be if you were forced to take a decision to act right now without any further information or consideration.
- Repeat the exercise and start with the same situation before any decision has been made. Spend time thinking through all the possibilities and options as to what might happen in the future. You can seek more information and talk to anyone to find out more. At what point do you feel ready to make the decision? Is anything holding you back?

- Think about these two scenarios and decide what feels right for you and at what point you choose to act, based on the likely outcome. Do you get a sense of what it means to have "good timing"?
- Make a conscious effort to improve your timing in relation to any changes or decisions which you might face in the future.

CHAPTER SIX: PAIN RELIEF

6.1   When Tragedy Strikes

Things can happen in life which may have a devastating effect and throw all our emotions up in the air. When this happens it is impossible to think that we will we ever feel any different to the way we do now. It might seem as if our lives are ruined and we must resign ourselves to the fact that we will never experience that sense of carefree happiness again.

Our concerns can be heightened if we are parents and this affects our children. It is natural to want to protect them from any exposure to pain and suffering. We worry that they may indeed be damaged for life if they experience a major trauma, especially if it is because of something we have brought on ourselves and the family, such as divorce or separation, and we may feel a huge sense of responsibility and guilt.

In all these situations it is important to remember that the reasons why we feel good about the world are because of own emotions and what they are telling us. Most people think that there is a prescription for happiness and that all the pieces are outside of ourselves and need to be in place before we can experience it. If we don't have them we chase after them and are convinced we won't be happy until we get them. It's almost as if we rely on the medicine of possessions to make us better. When we suffer physical disease the drugs are never guaranteed, and at the end of the day our own body has to take action to restore health. Providing someone with all the things which go with a certain lifestyle can help to induce happiness, but that is all. Taking something away may be traumatic but it is not necessarily the disaster we might think, since happiness is not produced by things in world outside but generated from within.

After the loss of something or someone important in life a period of adjustment will be needed and regaining a positive outlook can take time.

Most people invest or store their feelings in something outside of themselves and when they lose this valuable item they have also lost the triggers which allow them to connect and release positive emotions. The world feels empty and there is nothing to replace it. This is why bereavement can leave some people feeling numb. Once we realise what is happening here we can reassure ourselves that we will not feel like this forever if we take steps to address it. We need to make the most of opportunities to build new connections with other things, or even within ourselves, knowing that happiness is inside us. It is simply out of reach for now. Other things or triggers which might awaken this happiness don't have to be perfect. It's a question of making the best of what comes our way. The sooner we can do this the sooner we regain our positive outlook.

Continuing to mourn the loss of something or someone is not doing them any good, and if we can move on it does not mean that we are devaluing their importance. Their memory and the happiness they brought into our lives will always be cherished. We have not lost them as the connections will always be there. It is our job to make new ones, and there is no limit to the number we can create. The richest lives are those with the ability to make the greatest number of connections.

When Tragedy Strikes – Putting it into practice

KEEP IN MIND

- There is no prescription for happiness; we don't need things to make us happy. It's always inside us if we can find ways to connect with it.
- People generally invest their feelings in people and things outside of themselves and when they disappear they have lost the triggers which release these feelings of joy and happiness.
- It's important to build new connections and make the most of what comes our way.
- Continuing to mourn the loss of something or someone doesn't mean we devalue their importance. The connections remain, even when we move on and make new ones.

Quick Exercise:

- You have received a call from the police telling you that you have been burgled. Think of the three most important things which you hope have not been taken or destroyed. You have no money or means to replace them so if you have lost them you will never get them back.
- Notice how it feels not to have these items in your life.
- Choose one or more items which you use, or have contact with on a regular basis, and value.
  Lock them away out of sight for at least a week and notice how you respond. What does it feel like to be without them?

In Depth Exercise:

- Think back to a time when you experienced the loss of someone or something which was important to you.
- How did this person or thing make you feel about yourself and how did you feel when they were no longer there?
- Have you been able to find other ways to feel good about yourself and how easy was it to transfer the need to find new connections or triggers to provide you with the chance to feel good about yourself?

- Did you feel a sense of guilt when you moved on and stopped thinking about them?
- Are you able to love them without needing them?

6.2   Is it "them and us" or "we"

If you have a strong sense of "them and us" you may think that it's important to protect your family, your home and your lifestyle from the big forces and aggressive energies out there which you sense are always trying to break in and capture your hard-earned treasures.

This attitude can be exhausting, and you can easily feel threatened, with little energy left to have fun and enjoy things in a spontaneous way. When you feel this way, trying out new ideas and relationships may be seen as a risky business and not worth the effort.

Since our subconscious is what really controls us it is important to realise that we are very much influenced by instinct and emotion. These instincts and emotions are shared by all of humanity, albeit with different emphasis here and there, but on the whole we can all recognise their language. This means that most of us have the ability to empathise, and therefore communicate with each other, by sharing a sense of connection, even if we are meeting a total stranger for the first time. These connections are greatly increased when we are similar, such as sharing a lifestyle, ideology or occupation with someone, and the more in tune we are with their thoughts, feelings and responses, the greater the connection. Have you heard someone talk about their partner saying "I can read them like a book?" This is why we enjoy the company of friends who share common interests and ways of thinking as it enables us to feel a strong sense of knowing and therefore of connection. Developing common interests and keeping them going is a way to keep these connections open. The modern lifestyle often means that many people today do not experience this very strongly. They live a separate life and have little contact with the outside world. Living alone reinforces this sense of isolation and it becomes a vicious circle. They lose the connection with others and no longer feel comfortable going out. Their walls have been well and truly strengthened and anything beyond it feels hostile.

Once we find a way to lower those walls it becomes easier to drop the defences and open up to the outside world.

The feeling of connection which this brings is enough to dispel the sense of isolation and fear that we experience in protecting our egos.

One way to bridge this gap instantly is to give to others, whatever that gift might be. It is also an outward sign of the recognition of a greater self and allows the exchange of energies to begin. Such a feeling is life-changing. It recognises that we are much greater than we think we are, and this allows us to tap into the huge pool of energy and joy, rather than trying to meet our needs from the little puddle we have captured, spending the rest of our life protecting it for our own individual use.

Is it "them and us" or "we" – Putting it into practice

KEEP IN MIND

- Connections are important as they give us a sense of belonging to something bigger than our individual selves.
- Common interests and lifestyles help to build these connections.
- Isolation is a vicious circle; it weakens the links, creates hostility and builds barriers.
- Giving is an excellent way to build bridges. This exchange recognises our connection with others and gets the energies and positive emotions flowing again.
- Those who have a number of different interests and more contacts with people generally have a richer lifestyle and enjoy life more than those who are isolated.

Quick Exercise:

- Decide that you are going to give a stranger, or someone who is not a close friend or relative, a small gift with no expectation as to the outcome. This can be an item, or simply a smile or gesture of goodwill.
- Notice the feelings you get when you do this and notice the response in the person you are giving to.
- Do you feel any differently towards them after this "act of random kindness"?

In Depth Exercise:

- Do you have a particular hobby or interest and do you know others who share this?
- What are your thoughts and feelings about them as people? Do you find it easier to connect with them, rather than with someone who doesn't share the same interests as you?
- If you are feeling isolated and maybe slightly hostile towards the world can you think of any group, organisation or individual involved in the same activities and aspirations which interest you. What opportunities are there for you to join them in some way?
- How does it feel once you have become involved in a shared activity with this group or person?

6.3   Your demons are inside you

Everyone has problems and some people seem to be struggling with more than their fair share.   You may have noticed that people carrying a huge burden often sense trouble around every corner and feel that it's not possible to go through life without being caught up in a web of negativity.

I won't deny that there are a host of difficult situations in the world, and for many there are horrors which no-one can dismiss. However, the horror is always what you make of it.

A young woman asked me recently how she could avoid all those people in life who give her problems. She explained that she attracts the bully like a moth to the flame and thinks that she is easily manipulated. My immediate response was that it would be impossible to avoid them and the only way to deal with troubles of this sort is to acknowledge that they exist. The important focus however is to have some control over how it might affect you.

When a person is caught up in their own issues they cannot invest time in reflection.   Allowing the mind to gently explore, without worrying about the consequences, will reveal much more about the world and those who have the freedom to think like this are likely to gain a better understanding of how others might see the world differently.   When we start to put ourselves in someone else's shoes, with an objectivity that has very little judgement associated with it, we can begin to understand them. When we understand them we know what their motivation is, and when we know this we can start to see how they might behave towards us and what motivates them. This is very useful knowledge as it enables us to avoid or deal more easily with situations which cause pain and difficulty by realising the issue lies with them and not with us. The idea is not to judge these people but simply to respond in a way which does not allow us to become their victim.

The same applies to all circumstances in life.

Understanding the dynamics of all people and situations, with non-judgemental attention, leads to wisdom which enables us to respond appropriately, both to protect ourselves from being a victim and to falling prey to our own negative emotions.

It also helps the person inflicting the hurt or problem deal with it and move on.

The other important point to remember, and I can't emphasize this enough, is to accept that any pain and suffering we may be feeling is due to our own response; it is not because of the situation we are facing.

If we can acknowledge that our feelings create the pain, and then realise that we have some control over these feelings and reactions, we are on our way to a better life.

Your demons are inside you – Putting it into practice

KEEP IN MIND
- **Problems are impossible to avoid but we can have some control over how they affect us.**
- **Pain comes from our responses and not the problem itself.**
- **Understanding the motives of others through non-judgemental observation gives us a sense of freedom and choice over how we respond. There is never a good reason to feel like a victim.**
- **The way others might behave is their problem and not ours.**

Quick Exercise:
- Think about an incident in the last few weeks where someone was unpleasant, mean or even cruel towards you.
- Consider how you reacted to this.
- Reflect on what might have been going on with them and the challenges they might have been facing. There is never a good excuse for treating others badly but sometimes it's easier to understand when you know why that person is behaving the way they are.
- Accept that the problem is with them and not with you. Don't allow yourself to respond with anger and hurt and then lay the blame at their door.

In Depth Exercise:
- Do you remember a time when you felt unhappy and blamed others for the way you were feeling?
- Write down a list of all the feelings you remember during that period; how you felt about yourself and about those who you held responsible. This can often be people who have played an important role in your life, like parents, teachers, best friends, partners or bosses.
- With hindsight, can you see any reason why they might have behaved in that way?
- Accept that the way you feel is ALWAYS your responsibility. You can choose how you think and feel about any situation; you are the one in control.

- Remind yourself of this whenever you feel you are slipping into the mode of blaming others.

6.4   Acting "as if"

Sometimes we think our problems would vanish and our pain disappear if it wasn't for other people. We struggle to have any influence over them and are left feeling powerless and vulnerable.

It's true that there is often very little we can do to change the course of someone else's thinking, especially if we challenge them or put up an argument, as they will become defensive and refuse to listen to anything we are saying.

There is one important and very useful thing we can do however, and this can start to have a ripple effect which stimulates change in others and in our relationship with them. It's very simple and doesn't take a lot of effort or clever thinking on our behalf, in fact animals are often the best catalyst in stimulating change using this technique, with amazingly powerful results.

The answer lies in treating people as if they were pleasing to us, even when they are not. Most people are programmed to respond to others in a way which they think others expect. We often have a different face or persona depending on which group of people we are with as we want to live up to their expectations. We think this is because they would be disappointed, confused or even angry if we were not what they expect us to be, and the majority of us hate to be have these kinds of feelings directed at us. If they act as if they don't know us we end up feeling like we don't know ourselves. That sense of chaos is one of our biggest fears. Even cruel and sadistic people expect their victims to be scared and cowering. It introduces a completely different dynamic when we give back a positive response and this can interfere with the patterns and predictable behaviours which our persecutor might be repeating, often in a continuous feedback loop which is subconscious.

I don't want to suggest that anyone goes overboard and acts in a way which is ingratiating or clearly unbelievable to others. This will only cause friction and disbelief.

If we hold back from our immediate, and often negative response, and use this energy to visualise the person behaving in a way which we consider to be kind and generous towards us it will put an immediate brake on the escalation of negative energies between ourselves and the other person. We are no longer reflecting back their own negative feelings. We have put up a thought shield, deflecting their own feelings and stopping them from discharging onto us.

We all use other people to mirror and discharge our feelings, often affirming and accentuating them when others provide this affirmation by reflecting back to us what we are projecting onto them. If we change the message altogether all those involved are forced to stop and re assess what the world is now telling them. Depending on how strongly we feel, and how confident we are in these feelings, the change in us can be all that's needed to reverse the flow.

This exercise sounds simple but it can be very difficult to achieve. Firstly we are all a victim of our emotions and find that we cannot always stop the way we feel when someone pushes our buttons. It takes a lot of practice. Some of us are so caught up in these feelings we have no room for manoeuvre. Others who regularly stand back and use more control over their thoughts may have a moment to reflect before modifying their response. Even better, we may be able to exert full control over our behaviour by keeping our own thoughts as positive as possible at all times, without dwelling on anger, pain and hurt. Much depends on the situation we are in and the degree to which others can trigger our emotions or touch on particularly sensitive issues.

Practising this technique will give you more opportunity to use it effectively and once you have observed the results for yourself I am confident that you will be inspired to continue.

Acting "as if" – Putting it into practice

KEEP IN MIND
- There is very little we can do to change someone else's thinking.
- A very simple technique of acting "as if" can work wonders, but it takes practice and patience to achieve.
- Treat people as if they were pleasing to us, even if they are not.
- This can interfere with their usual responses and requires them to re-assess.
- We are all conditioned to reflect back what others present to us.

Quick Exercise:
- Next time you are receiving a hostile reaction from someone, stop and think before responding. Get a grip on your feelings and turn your thoughts around so that you are able to respond in a pleasant and friendly manner without being ingratiating or sarcastic.
- Note what happens and observe their reactions carefully.

In Depth Exercise:
- Do you have a bad relationship with someone in your immediate circle? How often does any form of communication between you both end in hostile feelings?
- Spend time on a regular basis visualising this person in a positive way. See yourself responding to them as if you were good friends. Remember all the things you may have said to them in the past and visualise new ways of communicating by reframing your words and actions in a positive light.
- Is there something you could do which would demonstrate this new approach towards them and require them to reassess?
- Try out some of these techniques when you see or speak to them again and note what happens.

CHAPTER SEVEN: BIG QUESTIONS

7.1   What's written on your tombstone?

No great piece of orchestral music is ever achieved without the conductor, who has overall control and makes sure all the different instruments play their part, resulting in a harmonious and pleasing sound. Without an overriding aim, or leading edge idea as to what we want in life, there will be a number of thoughts pulling us in different directions, with the inevitable challenges and conflicts which occur when different values struggle to get the upper hand.

The leading edge idea is not necessarily a static role, taking on a particular shape or form, but may simply be a sense of direction. More details may reveal themselves as life unfolds. For some this can be religion, although this is a word I really want to avoid as it can have some very negative connotations, suggesting control and keeping to the rules without question. Maintaining an overall sense of direction at the forefront of our life is something which each person must decide and develop for themselves. It really doesn't matter how we describe it since it is the feeling or intention which is all important, whether this is a more prescriptive set of principles or simply a sense of purpose.

If you don't think you have one then it is more than likely that you pick and choose from a whole range of ideas as the mood takes you. Perhaps you are influenced by the fashions and ideas of the day or follow in the footsteps of your family and friends. This can lead to contradiction, confusion and dissatisfaction, especially if you are trying to fulfil too many of them at the same time.

One analogy which illustrates this approach is a tendency to channel hop. Whilst it's good to be selective in what we choose to engage in, and review the options on a regular basis, there is always the danger that we never really appreciate the messages behind the pictures until we give the programme a chance to tell its story.

Understanding only comes if we spend time and energy focussing on the meaning behind it.

Maybe the theme is not a happy one and the ending is sad, but the consequences of our actions will only become clear if we allow the story to play out to the end. Only our experiences can provide us with information which can shape our decisions about what to do next.

The stronger our sense of direction the more focused we are in delivering our core beliefs, and the more we will be able to achieve them despite the odds. If this feeling is really strong we can deliver huge success but it has to be properly embedded in the mind so that it can work with other ideas and influences. A word of warning here; if greed and a self- serving attitude is our only aim it may be that we are very successful in delivering the outcomes we desire. However, this does not mean that it is in the best interest of the self or others.

It might seem like an attractive idea to be admired as a hero but being the champion of a leading edge idea may come at a huge personal cost. We may find ourselves a slave to the role itself, losing the chance to fulfil our potential in other areas as we rush headlong into achieving the goals set out for us without realising all the consequences. Next time you meet someone who doesn't seem quite rational, consider whether they may be identifying with a role to the exclusion of all else.

Whether we are fully signed up to the role or not, certain extras maybe added in as part of the package, whilst other personality traits maybe subdued or taken away. It's surprising how much effort we might apply in trying to change unwanted aspects of ourselves, but as these are now so much a part of the type of person we have become they are well and truly attached. Changing the leading edge idea is often the only way to loosen their grip.

Another pitfall is when we develop a leading edge idea which is too prescriptive, and is therefore subject to failure because it will be much harder to achieve.

If ideas are too well defined they will not allow spontaneity or flexibility. We will let opportunities slip by as they don't quite fit the brief or meet our expectations and we won't allow ourselves to go with the flow. This leads to disappointment and disillusion and we lose momentum.

The only way to decide whether our aims are in our long term interest is to measure how we would feel if everything was taken away from us, leaving us with nothing but the leading edge idea at the core of our being. The world cannot be ours forever and at some stage we will have to lose it, even if it happens through old age or death. How would we feel on our death bed, knowing we had spent most of our life chasing after this aim or objective?

The concept of an overriding principle, or leading edge idea, can also lead to conflict if it is at odds with others in society. The ideas and beliefs held by a group work in similar ways to those held by an individual. If there is an overarching value or principle to which all subscribe there will be success in delivering this, but if there is conflict neither the group nor the individual will function efficiently and harmoniously. We are delving into the field of politics here and this is the subject of another book.

Our exercise today can only go so far and talking about the big picture is a huge subject and one which I don't intend to explore right now. However, the answer to who, what and why is probably at the core of everyone's wellbeing. When the chips are down it may be the only thing that matters and when all the incidentals melt away you may find it has shaped the whole of your life and the choices you made without you even realizing it. All I would say here is that if you feel inclined to search for a deeper meaning I would recommend reading as widely as possible and when you find a common truth popping up in everything you read or come across, trust your judgement and congratulate yourself – you have begun the journey and started to find what you are looking for.

What's written on your tombstone? - Putting it into practice

KEEP IN MIND
- Sign up to one overriding leading edge idea and harmony reigns.
- All we need is a sense of direction. Let the details take care of themselves; being too prescriptive means that we miss opportunities by insisting on a perfect fit.
- Be aware of the consequences of following a leading edge idea and change if it doesn't feel right for you.
- Too many conflicting ideas mean chaos and confusion.
- Imagine you have nothing left but the ideas which shaped your life; how would the world remember you?

Quick Exercise:
- Write down three things or ideas which most closely describe your sense of direction and what you might consider to be most important to you right now in influencing your life.
- Rank them in order of priority ie which ones have most influence in shaping your decisions.
- Do they work well together or are they pulling in different directions?

In Depth Exercise:
- Imagine you have a short time to live. Look back over your life and decide what you might feel proud of and whether there is anything which makes you feel ashamed. Concentrate on these things and consider whether there is a word or phrase which sums up a leading edge idea which resulted in your actions, something which may have influenced you to become what you are today.
- Try and put these ideas into words so that the world can remember you for who and what you are. It may be useful to imagine this as the inscription on your tombstone.

7.2   Breaking the rules

How many times do you compare your own life with that of your friends and neighbours? We are constantly weighing up our lot and making comparisons with who has what, based on the values of society. If we think the scales are tipping in our direction we are satisfied, and if they look empty in comparison to others like us we are unhappy. Much of the time our happiness switch is determined by these comparisons, regardless of whether we really want what is on the scales or not. It is rare to take a long hard look at the items and goals which society considers we should all want and then make our own decisions about whether they are what we need to make us happy. Nine times out of ten they will not deliver this, but it can be hard to measure the items which really count.

If you are one of those people obsessed with weighing your lot, give some thought as to how you allow the opinions of society to affect your peace of mind. Remind yourself of this when you start ruminating about "how lucky so and so is" and "why can't I have that too", a very common mental trap which is only too prevalent in our daily lives.

Freedom belongs to those who can keep some distance between themselves and the voices of envy. These voices may be nothing more than the pressures of society, pushing all its members to fit in and sign up to a social norm in order to keep everyone in their place, wanting the same things and behaving in the same way. Having said that, societies do need to function effectively and people do need to live and work together in mutual co-operation. A degree of harmony is achieved by shared values, and signing up to a shared value system is important so it should not be rubbished completely.

The important thing here is that we keep our eyes open as to what is going on and realise that we can break the "rules" if we need to.

Looking at things with a sense of humour is valuable and having some compassion for those trapped in envy is of benefit.

This allows us to have a degree of choice over what we want and don't want.

Our happiness is paramount, and if we are not happy, let's think carefully about what we are chasing after in order to achieve this.

Breaking the rules - Putting it into practice

KEEP IN MIND

- **Comparing ourselves with others makes us forget everything in the rush to possess what we might consider to be our fair share.**
- **Once we get this share is it what we really want?**
- **Freedom belongs to those who can ignore the voices of envy.**
- **Choose what you feel is important in life and don't let society decide for you.**

Quick Exercise:

- Write down up to ten items which you really wanted and worked hard to possess. They could be items you already own or things you have achieved.
- Consider what the driving forces were in getting these items and what made you go after them.
- Think about whether they make you happy or whether other motives were behind possessing them.
- Now choose up to ten items which make you happy regardless of how you came by them.
- What value would the world place on these items?

In Depth Exercise:

- Take a blank sheet of paper and draw a line down the middle.
- On the left you are going to write down all the things you are chasing after and hoping to own or achieve one day.
- On the right you will write down all the things that you really feel will make you happy in life.
- See if there are any differences in the two lists and if so why.
- Look at the list on the left and consider what has influenced you in wanting to achieve or possess them.
- Spend time focusing on the list of things on the right which you feel will make you happy and ask yourself whether you are living your life in a way which is likely to deliver them.

7.3   Shared values

If you have worked through these exercises so far and started to take on board the ideas in this book you may be well on the way to getting some control over your mind. Your thoughts maybe more positive, rewarding and creative, you may have better control over the way you respond to events and people without being sucked into a whirlpool of emotion, and you may find yourself getting up in the morning with a sense of joy and anticipation, rather than foreboding or even dread. But what about the rest of the world and all the people in your life; are they oblivious to the changes they see in you?   Even if they know nothing about what might be creating change in your life you are definitely going to have an effect on them. We are all so tightly interlinked our every action is governed and influenced by other people in both practical and emotional ways. Society is a big influence in determining what we can do, how we can do it and how we feel once we have done it. Even the hermit alone on the desert island uses words in order to frame ideas and feelings and these words have been created by society.

When you realise how interlinked every thought and action is you will appreciate the impact we have on others. The way we think, feel and act never goes unnoticed and as we go about the world as positive thinking, controlled and considerate people this will create a reaction in everyone we meet. We all mirror others and respond accordingly.   Actions do speak louder than words. Ideas and thoughts develop around them and percolate throughout society. When enough people begin to take on board a way of thinking it will affect many more, even if the majority had no intention or motivation to seek change for themselves and are largely unaware of the forces acting on them. The difficulty comes in starting out as one individual and then keeping the faith. It certainly helps if we surround ourselves with like-minded people, as our joint efforts will be magnified and we can build a head of steam until something unusual is accepted as something common-place. Then the rest of the world may follow.

This is the new revolution which could change the way we evolve.

Change comes from changing who we are, rather than trying to apply ideas like sticking plaster, pasting over the cracks and hoping no one will see the conflicts, insecurities and confusion we are really feeling. It's so easy to get bogged down in all the unsettling aspects and questions associated with change and much easier to stay in our comfort zones, avoid tension and not rock the boat. However, change is really easy if we let it happen and don't force the issue in any way. All that is required is that we remember three simple words: **Like attracts like**. Put out there what we think and feel and let the law of attraction do the work for us. Momentum will build and the snowball gets so big no one can stop it. If we try and force our agenda and push ideas onto others who are not thinking along the same lines as we are, resistance will occur and the only reaction we get is defensiveness and hostility. No-one can expect to win everyone over but the chances of success are certainly much higher if we work on ourselves in order to become happy, fulfilled individuals rather than pretending to be something or someone we are not.

Let your success speak for itself. Everyone is searching after happiness and looking for answers in the outside world. If they see you have achieved it they will want to share your secret.

Shared values – Putting it into practice

KEEP IN MIND
- **Whatever we do, say or think will have an effect on others.**
- **Like attracts like.**
- **Surrounding ourselves with like-minded peoples can strengthen our resolve.**
- **Change comes from within. It's easy if we hold fast to our ideas and let them happen, rather than trying to force our thoughts on others.**

Quick Exercise:
- When you are involved in a discussion about an issue or debate, try giving a clear definite response about how you think and feel in a calm and friendly way and avoid argument.
- Note the response you get from others.
- If a similar opportunity arises again, try a more argumentative and judgemental approach. Insist that others listen to your ideas and claim that you are right.
- Compare this with the first response.
- Appreciate how easy it is to find like-minded people to share ideas with, and how much better you can progress these ideas when you have clear and positive thoughts and the confidence to express them without the need to prove yourself.

In Depth Exercise:
- Think of a new idea or activity which you are interested in but have not yet discussed with anyone else. Ideally it should be something fairly unusual or novel which others may not have considered. Who would you like to share this with and why?
- Note the reaction of those you tell. Compare how you feel with someone who expresses interest or gives you support and encouragement, rather than with those who brush you aside or don't seem interested.
- Try out different ways of talking about your idea, and who you decide to share it with, and see what works best.

7.4 Like ice in the sun

Sometimes we want to own something or become someone so that we can enjoy a sense of relief and pride in the fact that we appear to have achieved success. Much of our energy is used in trying to prove that we are better than our neighbour, or have gained a reputation for being someone important. Once we have the things we crave we believe that we are no longer considered to be a nothing or a no-body and therefore we will be protected from all manner of threats from the outside world. Unfortunately this feeling is usually short lived once we realise that the security blanket we were so proud of is beginning to slip away.

Nothing lasts forever since everything is in a constant state of change. The world and all the things that we struggle to possess may appear solid but this is an illusion. If we could speed up time this process of change would be all too visible. The material world and all our experiences are like patterns of ice which appear on the window, only to melt away when the temperature rises. It doesn't matter how complex, intricate and solid, these structures might appear to be right now, their time is limited.

For some people this knowledge brings a sense of relief as they realise that their problems will not last forever. Others cannot bear to think they will lose all the lovely things they have worked so hard to achieve or rely on for their well-being. The important thing to bear in mind is that we can never possess anything or anyone forever, not even our own life.

Although all things are temporary the information which creates the framework behind their existence is not. If conditions are right these things will emerge again in much the same way as frost re-appears when the temperature drops. These patterns are like a set of instructions based on the rules of mathematics and this information is at the heart of all things. Once you start looking you can see how patterns crop up everywhere and are evident in a whole range of things. A typical example is the shape and structure of trees, the tributaries of rivers, the blood vessels in the body and in flashes of lightning.

Human beings learn to recognise patterns from an early age in order to make sense of the world. Without this ability we would never learn to read, write or even speak.

Maybe we need to spend longer looking for the patterns behind all things, rather than putting value on the things themselves which we then try to capture by believing that we can own them forever. Wisdom comes from understanding these patterns. We cannot own wisdom, but it's something we can all share, and something which is never lost.

Like ice in the sun – Putting it into practice

KEEP IN MIND
- Being a nothing or a no-body is scary; we all want the comfort of being recognised, either by owning possessions or enjoying attributes and abilities.
- Speed up time and you will see how quickly things appear and disappear. Nothing lasts forever and change is constant.
- We can never really own or possess anything, even our own lives.
- The patterns or rules which shape things and bring them into existence remain. Let's spend more time understanding these patterns, rather than trying to own the things themselves.
- Wisdom is something we can all enjoy, achieve and share.

Quick Exercise:
- Think of a situation which is constantly changing. You might like to choose the growth of a plant or the way the seasons change.
- Notice how everything in nature is moving and never stands still. If you could speed up time the changes would become very noticeable.
- Appreciate how one thing leads on to another and how everything goes in cycles.

In Depth Exercise:
- Take a look at your own life and select a particular aspect or situation where you feel fed up or stuck.
- See if you can identify small changes which have taken place and then apply the fast forward button to speed up time.
- Notice how the pace of change speeds up too and start to appreciate how everything is constantly moving and how impossible it is to stand still.
- Be prepared to go with the flow. Don't try and hang on to any situation now that you realise movement and change are inevitable.
- Look for patterns in things and place more value on them than the things themselves. Realise that patterns give shape to energy and

without energy nothing would exist. Reality is nothing more than shapes in the sand when the wind has passed over it. This appreciation is wisdom.

WHAT NEXT….

I hope you enjoyed reading through this book and thinking about some of issues it raises. Maybe you have tried out some of the exercises and come face to face with things you never realised about yourself and others. Some of you may be inspired by what you have read and find it has triggered thoughts of your own, or simply confirmed what you already know but never seem to have time to put into practice. Others may be feeling puzzled and confused, or struggling to get thoughts and ideas into some sort of order.

The world can certainly be a confusing and challenging place, and there are no easy answers to many of the questions we live with today. Perhaps we may only reach a conclusion once the issues have worked themselves through, but from where we are standing right now it's impossible to guess what the outcome will be. Even when we know the outcome, what is considered right by one person may be seen as wrong by another. It all depends on our point of view, and these viewpoints are many and varied. Like shifting sands each one is constantly changing, and the world itself never stands still. Being right or wrong is never a meaningful phrase as it depends on who is doing the judging.

A useful way to try and understand what is going on in the world, and in ourselves, is to look at nature. It offers so many examples about how the world works, and by observing these processes we can explain the dynamics behind so many things. For example, our feelings can be so much easier to grasp if we use the analogy of weather. Language and conversation are full of words and phrases, such as feeling under the weather, feeling calm, experiencing a raging temper. In this book you may have noticed how I have also used analogies such as comparing our mind with a garden to understand better how thoughts take root in the same way as plants.

We can cultivate a beautiful garden with the help of the right plants, choosing carefully to suit the conditions, giving them the nutrients they require, getting rid of weeds and pests and providing the care and attention which each one needs to thrive.

In the same way we can nurture certain thoughts and ideas whilst weeding out others. We may also look at how certain species or thought forms compete for dominance, how patterns made by frost and crystals are triggered by external factors in the same way that patterns and prejudices of behaviour repeat when the environment is favourable for them to manifest. The list is endless, and once we appreciate how many things are governed by the same underlying patterns we can spot them everywhere.

Whatever your response, I hope that you now have questions and yet more questions. We only learn when our curiosity is aroused and there is never going to be a time when questions are not needed. Human beings are the pioneers of unexplored territory; maybe our only purpose is to push forward into the unknown and learn from our experiences. As we do so we leave a trail of information behind. From where we stand right now, this data gets more and more complicated. As the speed of change increases, more and more combinations take shape as a result of our thoughts and actions. However, there is an underlying pattern or dynamic which begins to show through in all forms of manifestation and once we become aware of this we have a way out of the maze.

It is the consequences of change and our responses to it which shape the future, and if we want to find a way to make the journey easy and pleasant we need to pay attention to these consequences so that we choose a path which offers us a happier future.

None of us know where the path might end, if at all, but we should all aim to have fun on the way and do our best to leave some useful tips for those following on behind.

Now that you have reached the end of the ME FIT handbook you may have some useful comments; writing a review is always very much appreciated.

Those who would like to continue with the mental fitness training, either independently or with others, can find more information, including ideas and updates, on the ME FIT website.

www.mefittraining.com

Whilst inner dialogue and developing the relationship with ourselves is what it's all about, some may find their experiences are enriched by doing the exercises in a group. This can stimulate new ideas and allow us to see things from a different perspective. It is also a great way to get to know people better and have fun. Why not try it out with a few friends, or sign up to a more structured workshop programme with a facilitator?

Templates are available on the website to assist with carrying out many of the exercises, either in a group or independently.

Do use the contact us page to tell us about your progress and experiences and we will aim to respond.

23288460R00066

Printed in Great Britain
by Amazon